I0419948

THE QUICK AND EASY STEPS TO WRITING A NOVEL FOR FICTION WRITERS AND NOVELIST

By Jack Roberts

Table of Contents

CHAPTER 1:
THE CRUCIAL ELEMENTS OF A NOVEL

PLOT

Plot is the events that structure a story, particularly: as they communicate to one another in a sequence or in a pattern; as they relate to one another through cause and effect; how the reader understands the story; or simply by chance. Authors are mostly interested in how sound this pattern of events completes some emotional or artistic effect. A complicated, intricate plot is known as an imbroglio, but even the modest statements of plot may consist of multiple inferences, as in old-fashioned ballads. A plot is composed of causative events, which are a succession of sentences connected by and so. A plot highlights the important ideas and the line of a story. Ansen Dibell writes: Plot is built of important events in a particular story – significant because they have crucial consequences. Consequently, it has the same meaning with storyline.

Importance of Plot

- A book that's too mechanical is unsatisfying

- Thrillers normally follow a set pattern: climax, set-up, detective work and denouement.

- The consequence of the plot is the resolution of the matter that keeps you in your seat.

- The backbone of a plot is the piece— the major element that makes the audience/reader wants to stay until the end.

- Plot is what creates something literature as faced with real life — while real life meanders on, plot is definitely structured.

- Plot is not essential; considers plays like 'Waiting for Good'. A novel/play might have an objective instead of a plot.

- Must a plot have "a starting, middle and an end?" Not certainly.

- It is what occurs; the story.

- It is the vortex; everything middle on it and comes out of it, it is filled with twists and turns.

- It is the controlling force that moves the story.

- It is a structure and a sequence of events that move the story from starting to end.

- It is a logical means to create ideas on which to suspend characters.

- A beginning, middle and an end, but not certainly in that order.

What makes a good Plot?

- It contains good scenes in which 'good characters' create 'good speeches' based on 'good ideas'.

- It has a solid story-line.

- It contains a mystery or intrigue that readers want to solve.

- It's vivid but not predictable or simplistic; easy to follow, however engaging enough to make readers/listeners want to hear or read again.

- It uses conflicting moods, characters, settings etc. as a means of evoking listeners'/ readers' memories and playing with their emotions.

- It is consistent and credible in terms of characters, locations and style and how they communicate to the action.

- It contains 'surprises', e.g. in terms of unexpected characters or events behaving unexpectedly.

- It contains some elements of conflict; possibly resolved — possibly not.

- It contains at least some elements of uniqueness.

- It expresses a clear message(s) to the listener /reader, even though the message of the piece is an unsettled issue.

- It doesn't control the other abilities of the piece, such as characterization.

- The main elements of the plot are memorable.

SETTING

The setting in which your story takes place is such a crucial part of your book. The place and time can set the tone from the very beginning. Your setting should be developed in a way a character would be developed. If you think about books like the Lord of the Rings series or Harry Potter, the setting could be explained as another, very dominant character in the story. Thorough research of the location and time of your story, together with characters that will also act and dress properly throughout the book, is the solution to engaging your reader. Sometime when making a story for a novel, the focus and excitement is mostly on plot and characters, but the significance of harmonizing your characters and plot with the story, lies in a realistic setting. That is why we have made setting one of the vital parts of the Now Novel procedure. If you make a decision that Italy is the correct place for your romance novel, be alert that readers will have quite good sense of what to be expecting, so be certain to get your details right. If fantasy world unfolds your story through the back of a wardrobe, feel free to make use of poetic license!

Do not just concentrate on the location but as well the period. Even in fantasy world there are elements that either will or will not be satisfactory to the books believability. Author Jody Hedlund's advice is to take care of how much you offer the reader. "Too much will bore a reader and make them to skim over needless facts. This is dangerous in historical novels which have been lengthily researched, and the author thinks they should all get in". Too little will deprive the reader of understanding what the characters are experiencing. An error often caused by plot driven writers who make use of too few details as they only concentrate on narrating the story, or where too little research has been carried out.

CHARACTER

Characterization in actual fiction has special significance, and authors need to widen their own sense of conscientiousness for full and efficient character development. Character is absolutely everything in actual fiction. it is not as if character replaces setting and plot or meaning and theme, but character closely relates to all those. Though characters are often categorized as flat or round, all characters in fiction must have uniqueness and complexities that may or may not be added on the page. A character that doesn't need to be totally presented for the story may seem two dimensional, but three dimensions should be in the creator's mind. Complete character development guarantees that the author has thought about the whole story as a unit. Deepness of understanding of the characters assures basic motivations are dialogue believable, logic of action is clear and reasonable.

The aim of character making in fiction is intricate, but making a unique character; one that's not stereotypical, is the real meaning of grand fictional stories. The character will be taken by the reader, and the characters will drive the impetus of the plot. At the beginning of character growth, there are no limitations. A character appears unencumbered. Then that character must be ideal for the plot. The character must be distinctive, but remain convincing and within the limitations set by the suspense of doubt all fiction necessitates. The character mustn't be stereotypical, nevertheless must feel comforting to the reader in a known way. As a memorable character develops, the reader becomes attached — and admires the character in the same way they would begin to like a new acquaintance as a friend. This reader attachment is often associated with liking the character, but affinity is not absolutely necessary. Respect and/or admiration are also strong attachments for a reader to a character. As the author creates an emerging character, subtle choices and imaginative attributes given to the character must keep within the overall story guidelines set in the contract between author and reader. Subsequently, in revision, scenes, thoughts, actions, conflicts and motivations that do not contribute maximally to the character engaging the reader and driving the plot forward are eliminated, or at least changed.

To create a character for a reader in an actual story, there are restricted numbers of things the character can do or think. In a brief story, even for the central character, there can be just ten to twenty key characterization opportunities. Sometimes, even fewer. In novel, with its longer timeline and wider collection of development from the straight story line, there are extra opportunities for a character to display his or her true colors, but eventually, these openings are restricted. How do authors obtain key opportunities and utilize them? Firstly, character development should be rational for the story and for the awareness of the reader. The thoughts and actions of the character should also be distinctive, with elements of surprise, to facilitate the traits and actions inserted in readers' memory. In-scene viewing of a character's actions, thoughts and opinions has more lasting impact than narrative telling. And character development drops more impression on the reader while in-scene story time outweighs narrator or back story comments on past character actions. Stories, to be great, should be important and meaningful. A chief way for an author to inspire these traits in storytelling is through efficient characterization.

NARRATION

Narration is the report of connected events, imaginary or actual, offered in a sequence of spoken or written words, or moving images or still. Narrative can be ordered in a number of formal and/or thematic categories: non-fiction (e.g. biography, definitively including creative non-fiction, historiography, and journalism); fictionalization of historical events (e.g. historical fiction, legend, myth, and anecdote); and fiction proper (e.g., or live or recorded performances, novels, such as short stories, and narrative songs and poems, as well as visual narratives as portrayed in other textual process, games, or poetry and sometimes literature in prose). Including speech, art, and entertainment, Narrative is seen in all systems of human creativity, literature, theatre, journalism, comics, song and music, radio, television and video, film, gameplay, unstructured recreation, and performance in general, as well as some painting, drawing, sculpture, photography, and other imaginary arts (though numerous modern art movements decline the narrative in approval of the conceptual and abstract), as long as a order of events is presented. The word is coined from the Latin verb 'narrare', to 'tell' which is coined from the adjective gnarus, 'knowing' or 'skilled'

Oral storytelling is possibly the earliest system for sharing narratives. Throughout most people's childhoods, cultural history, narratives are used to direct them on proper behavior, formation of a communal personality, and values, as particularly studied in anthropology today among indigenous peoples. Narratives also behave as 'living' entities throughout the cultural stories, as they are handed on from generation to generation. Because the narrative storytelling is sometimes left without explicit values, children behave as participants in the storytelling procedure by digging deeper into the open ended story and creating their own interpretations. The word 'story' may be taken as a synonym for 'narrative' as well as for 'plot', the combined events within any specified narrative. Narratives can also be nested inside other narratives, such as narratives told by an undependable narrator (a character) typically seen in noir fiction genre.

A significant part of narration is the narrative method, the set of methods used to relate the narrative through a procedure.

Along with exposition, description, and argumentation, is one of four rhetorical modes of discourse, broadly defined, narration. More closely defined, it is the fiction-writing mode where the narrator relates directly to the reader.

DIALOGUE

Dialogue is the most powerful tool available to fiction writers because of its adaptability and the quantity of jobs it can achieve. But before we develop to the eight reasons to practice dialogue, just let me a moment to weigh-in my suggestion on three dialogue problems. First, I am in agreement with Stephen King that 'adverbs are not your friends.' So I rather prefer to avoid -ly endings as dialogue highlighting whenever possible, she said shyly. Instead, I rather use descriptive beats, she said, violation the contact of their gaze. Second, my private preference is to stick mostly to the tag 'said'. Saying she giggled, laughed, murmured, growled, barked, shouted, coaxed, gets distracting, and raged and so forth. In contrast, the word 'said' is nearly invisible to readers. I sometimes have a character whisper and if you explore my stories you'll surely find an

–ly ending in there somewhere, but I actually think about it first. Third, try to restrict colloquial language, "Aare yaw'll luse yar r-r-reader, lassie. Ya ken?" Such speaking in moderation may increase realism, individuality and concern. But too much of a good thing is too much of a good thing. It's hard work to decode all that phonetic spelling. An alternative is to tell the reader initially on that the character has an accent and then mimicking the cadence of that dialect.

Reasons Dialogue is an Author's friend:

1. Dialogue Adds the Illusion of Actuality: Real people have discussions. Give your characters a realistic discussion is a brilliant way to create the look that your creations are breathing and living people.

2. Dialogue Makes Reading Cooler: Dialogue breakdown blocks of exposition with lots of appealing white space. I have seen readers flip through a book's pages before buying. So what are they looking for? They might check how fast the reading will go (white space).

3. Dialogue exposes Character: Dialogue can expose things about characters, level of

education, upbringing, about their habits, ethnic background, thoughts, faith and many other interesting and important facts. E.g.: 'You are worried.' 'Why do you say so?' 'You are grinding your teeth so they squeak."

4. Dialogue exposes Secrets: This is one of my absolute preferred uses of dialogue, hitting the reader right between the eyes with a secret they never expected. Revealing mysteries in dialogue gives them actual power and more element of surprise.

5. Dialogue exposes Relationships: You can learn more about characters about how they speak to one another other and what they chose to disclose, or hide, in dialogue.

6. Dialogue Displays Backstory: An experienced author knows more than to drop a large mass of block of backstory in exposition. Dialogue, on different view, is a great way to expose something significant about the characters history. Be watchful not to have double characters who both understand the past dialogue about something just for the reader's

benefit. This mostly comes across as unusual.

7. Dialogue Progresses the Story: Dialogue is a powerful way to keep things on motion, principally if new info comes to light, secrets are exposed or problems are intricate.

8. Dialogue Expand Conflict: There is no issue that an author can't make worse. Conversation is a great place to have two characters conflict over any number of disputes. It's exciting to hear people argue, especially if the conflict is about a belief or value. Be careful, though, protagonists who constantly argue. Characters that can't be in a room without fighting correctly making the reader marvel if they have what it takes to live as a couple.

OTHER CONSIDERATIONS

Genre

Genre is plot-driven fictional works written with the intent of fitting in a particular literary genre, in order to entreat to fans and readers already familiar with that genre. Genre fiction is usually distinguished from literary fiction. Robert McKee the screenwriting teacher defines genre conventions as the 'specific settings, events, roles, and values that define individual genres and their subgenres'. These conventions, are usually implicit, always fluid, but from time to time are made into explicit requirements by producers of fiction as a hint to authors seeking for publication. There is no consensus that is exactly what the conventions of any genre are, or even what the genres are; giving of works to genres in some extent subjective and arbitrary. Genre is often controversially discharged by literary critics as being clean escapism, clichéd, and of low quality prose.

Writing Style

Styles of writing refer to the manner in which an author takes to write to his or her readers. A style exposes both the writer's voice and personality, but it also displays how he or she notices the audience. The best of a conceptual writing style create the whole character of the work. This happens through changes in syntactical arrangement, adding diction, parsing prose, and establishing figures of thought into useful frameworks. Lot of writers are under the impression that in order to be a prosperous, they must create and promote their own characteristic and distinctive writing style, publish author, but the truth is by doing that, they could be cultivating bad habits instead. The truth is, writing styles are not rather sometimes that writers typically think about, but rather something that progresses naturally over time. Writing methods is as much to do with individuality which is about writing. It is all about how the writer offers the words to the reader, how well he or she recognizes the beauty of the language, how sound a fiction world or fictional characters are merged together, how each sentence starts and ends, how each paragraph is united with the narrative, how description and narrative are created. It is how well a writer tells their tale. In a way to force style into their writing, writers seem to be deliberately literary or arty, or even worse, they try to be ingenious. They do this by copying positively, writing styles of famous authors, little realizing the works for the popular author, does not certainly work for Joe Writer. That's where corrupt habits creep in, so purposefully making a writing style does not work.

Writers develop so as their writing style. A writer's work start becoming multidimensional and multifaceted, where before it may have been plane and uninspiring. The writer starts to notice a change in his or her work. There is an abundant force at work the more a writer literally writes – self-awareness. Become aware of the nature of the word which is written and understand the intricacy made through description is like a light bulb moment. That is because the writing style has come to a point where it stands out to the writer – it has progresses naturally. And once it happens, the writer will instinctively know because writing become nearly seamless and much cooler and the writer will become stress less with their work. It is only as significant as an individual need it to be. Style is all about originality and individuality. Often readers can find an author's exact style, whether that may be succinct and short, brash and gritty, colorful and lavish, or just plain quirky. And readers seem to like certain styles.

Length

how long should a chapter be? What is the best length? And does a novel have to fit in a set amount of words? These are just two most common questions asked by the writers. They presume they must have to work in a strict template of X amount of chapters and X amount of words, usually because most novels have about 30 or 40 chapters and about 80,000 words.

Novel Lengths

Firstly, let's removes a few myths - novel lengths are spoken by the story itself, not the editor or the writer or a particular written formula. Secondly, writers do not have to fit their word count in a generic set amount. Again, the story will tell how long the novel will be. It is also worth knowing the types of novels that work well with different word counts. Straightforward stories containing least characters tend to be short, typically around 20,000 to 60,000 words. These are known as novellas. Longer, more difficult stories, which consist of a handful of main and peripheral characters, tend to run at about 60,000 to 95,000 words. This would make up the average length novel. The saga – a lot of characters and an intricate, epic story told over several generations – think War and Peace - typically run at about 100,000 words.

If you're writing a standard length novel, aim for about 80,000 to 95,000 words. It does not have to be precise, but it is there to guide writers. If you place yourself at a target of 85,000 words, you will realize that if you go-amiss of that average figure, your story is either missing in substance, or it does not have enough energy to be a full length novel (without any serious editing), and would thus be a novella instead. If you go over that figure and you discover yourself drifting over 100,000 words, then you require to make some serious changes to reign the story back in, or else you risk it becoming a saga. Another reason to make use of these figures as a guide is to permit you submit your MSS to an agent or publisher affirming what kind of story it is, i.e. a thriller based novel which contains 150,000 words, you might get a rejection before anyone could even read the first line of the first chapter because that type of length for that kind of story just is not a viable option for them. Equally, if you state that you have an epic tale of revenge and love, set in the last century, which trails several generations of the same family, the editor would draw back at a paltry 75,000 words. In other words, consider the genre you are writing, think about the tale itself, and suppose what kind of book you are writing. Can it be told in that rational amount of words?

Chapter lengths

Writers will soon learn that there are no set rules when it comes to writing and chapter lengths. New writers are likely to presume that a chapter must have a certain set length for it to maintain the average novel length of about 80,000 to 95,000 words, but in reality, chapters can be as short or as long as you want them to be. There's no formula. You do not have to pick a number like 80,000 and then split it by 30 chapters to give you 2500 words a chapter (standard). If you have read Faulkner's "As I Lay Dying" or any Stephen King novels, then you will realize that a chapter can be a sentence long or even one word. It can also be 5000 words. yet again, like novel length, chapter length is ordered by what's happening in the story, not by the rule of averages and applied mathematics. A lot of books have 40, 50 or sometimes 60 chapters, all unstable in length. And it is the mixture of length that counts. They do not have to conform to any pre-determined ideas. Every writer is different; therefore every chapter they write will differ in length. The only thing you require to apply is where chapter lengths and novel lengths are concerned, it's common sense. If you suppose a chapter is far too short for any reason, inspect it to see why. It may be that you have not included adequate description. If your chapter appears to go on and on, look again to see if it's overly long - you risk boring your reader and losing their attention if it does not sagaciously move to the next chapter. If a thing like an average chapter exists, it would perhaps be around 2500 words. Or 10 x A4 sheets, because this also performs as a visual prompt for some people. There are no solid and fast rules. It is all down to the type of story you're writing, how you narrates it, and of course, a touch of common sense.

CHAPTER 2:
NOVEL WRITING HOW-TOs

HOW TO CHOOSE THE GENRE

Do you desire to sell thousands of copies of your novel? No matter the route you choose, your capacity to pick the correct genre for your novel can be the difference between success and anonymity. Genre is the kind of story you are writing. Most readers and booksellers recognize genres such as fantasy, romance, mystery, science fiction, historical, thriller, suspense etc.

Important of Genre

Editors and agents tend to concentrate on some specific genres. Lest your manuscript tallies with the genre an agent signifies, it will end up in the slush pile. Editors and agents use genre to see if you understand what you are writing. There is nothing an agent dislikes more than hearing "my book is a bit of a mystery, but it is set in a dystopian future, thus it is sort of sci-fi and there is a love story, so it is also kind of a romance" If you do not know the genre your book fits, you are saying you do not know your target audience. And without knowing your target audience, you will not be able to know how to market your book. This can make an agent reason twice about signing you, if you are adamant that 'you do not want to be labeled' because your book is 'so complex' well, that is a clear indication that you are more fascinated by your identity as an artist than you being a selling author.

What will make an agent decline you absolutely?

Your ideal audience uses genre in finding your book

Let us say you like mysteries.

You have got a long trip ahead. You have read all the books by your beloved authors, and you desire to read something new. When you get into any book store you are not going to wander aimlessly around the store. You will simply go straight to the mystery division. So if I have written a mystery but shelved it in the Romance section because the detective falls in love, you will not be able to find my book, because you were not looking there. And some poor romance readers will be annoyed because they were expecting a lot more romance, not solving-death issues. To be brief, choosing the correct genre is about refining your odds of making sale.

Here are four steps that will help you choose the right genre for your book:

1. Getting to know the genre options

A swift look at Amazon's Books page, or a visit to any bookstore, will enable you know the main classifications of fiction. Amazon bestseller page for book splits its list by genre.

Glance at the top five bestsellers in each genre. Recite each book explanation. What does each genre accentuate? E.g. James Patterson's NYPD Red 2 is on the list for "Thriller, Suspense & Mystery" The description structures shocking murders, brutal slaughter, and crime scenes

Now glimpse through the Romance list. 'Nora Roberts' The Collector' also involves resolving a murder. But it defines 'the woman with no perpetual ties finds herself nearly wishing for one' and 'Ash desires to paint her as passionately as he hungers to touch her.' The emphasis is obviously the passion within the protagonists rather than the resolution of the issue. Once you have looked through some book's description, you will understand which elements are most crucial to each genre's readers.

2. Recognize genre elements in your work

- Gaze closely at your novel.

- Does it contain a love story? Or a crime?

- Are there any elements of magic or the supernatural?

- Is it established in the past, present, or future?

- How old are the protagonists?

- What motivates the plot?

- You are looking for elements that could assist you narrow the focus.

- What do you think is most important in the book?

- What element do you enjoy the most? What makes you proud the most?

- You do not need to make a choice about genre yet. You are just searching for the story pieces that'll help you make the right choice. You have to know what you are working with.

- Once you have got a list of your story components, you are prepared to move to the next step.

3. Find your most likely reader

–   What kind of reader would like your novel, and why?

–   Have in mind that the question is not which readers may enjoy your novel. Anybody could buy the book by accident, and be astonished at how much they liked something outside their type.

–   But the odd of finding that person is slim. That is not marketing – it is luck.

–   Instead, you are targeting the fan that will go absolutely nuts for exactly what you have written.

–   Who's the screaming super fan for this book?

–   Try to picture a specific person.

–   Pretend you are reading a review by your super fan. What does it say?

–   Outside the generic "this book is amazing," what does the super fan precisely adore about your novel?

–   Its supple plot like Dan Brown suspense?

- Or maybe the thorough and complex world building, like Hugh Howey's Wool series?

- Or perhaps the toe-curling love scenes, like that of E.L. James' 50 Shades of Grey?

- What does your super-fan criticize?

- Have genre conventions in mind.

- If the couple in your love story pass away at the end, romance fans will be up in arms, since they expect a 'happily ever after' or at least 'happily for now' resolution.

- Dissatisfying a reader means poor sales and bad reviews.

- Be sure your super-fan is happy with the entire story, not just some parts of it.

4. Use reasonable titles to secure your sub-genre

Each genre expresses books by writers who offer diverse flavors – unlike sub-genres. Dan Green composes police procedurals in his Max Segal series. These are very unlike from the comfortable amateur sleuth of Jessica Beck's Donut Mysteries, or the erotic, silly fun of Janet Evanovich's Stephanie Plum series.In the new adult genre, there is a wide difference between dystopian love stories similar to The Hunger Games and Divergent, the fizzing Braced to Bite, and the angsts Twilight. When you know your most expected buyer, imagine you are observing an online bookstore sales page for your novel. Beneath the 'purchase' button you will find endorsements for other novels, thru the phrase "People who bought this also bought..."

Imagine three novels your super-fan might like that is similar to yours in content and style. Find where these are classified on Amazon or in your local bookstore. This is how you'll identify the genre that's suitable for your novel. Though you plan to publish, but learning how to pick the suitable genre for your novel is crucial. It'll teach you how to match the finest elements of your writing with the audience that'll most appreciate them. The better you get at detecting your reader and your strengths, the more accurately you will pick your novel's genre. And the more sales you will make.

HOW TO SET THE TONE

Setting the Tone

We act differently at a conference than we would while hanging out with friends, or at least we ought to. We act contrarily, because our aim is different. When we relate with others in a conference, we project our attitude through our body language; though, when we interact with others via email we project our attitude through tone. Exactly as the pitch and volume of one's voice transmits attitude and tone at meetings and parties, the choice of words and how way we put our sentences together express a sense of tone and attitude in our writing. Are we being serious or frivolous, casual or formal, stuffy or sweet? The choice of one word can alter the tone of an email. For example, the phrasal verb 'hanging out' conveys a diverse tone than other words we would have chosen like assembling, consorting, congregating, gathering, or fraternizing. When writing an email, consider tone. Estimate how you want to be acknowledged and how to arrange your message in such a way that you get the outcomes you want. When the incorrect tone is offered, the reader will be stuck up on how you made them feel, such as excited or offended, instead of getting the meaning of your email. Tone is approach, whether you want to be bold or subtle, tone is transported through word choice, sentence construction and even typestyle. Writing software can assist you hit just the right note.

Word Choice

After objectifying the results you want, reason about word choice. We sometimes get lazy in this area; don't forget that written language is different from spoken language. Slang or sarcastic language may not be received well in writing and unsuitable tone, such as aggressive or superficial diction, that the reader does not find funny, can destruct relationships and hinder development. Always think about who is getting your email before you send it and recall that emails are not secretive, many companies monitor and save email, so exercise cautiousness with casual communication.

When discerning about word choice, ethically correct is best. Avoid language that victimizes or makes assumptions. All sexist, racists, ageist or religious language should be dodged and correspondence should be inscribed with the global market in mind. A mistake in this area can create offence and sink the deal. Do not make assumptions, like 'everyone knows.' or 'I'm sure you consider this.' You may be wrong and easily offend readers with these types of speeches; additionally, no one wants you to tell them what they think. Dodge $10 words, except you know your reader knows the significance of these words. Occasionally we have a tendency to use intricate words when a more direct, modest word would work. If your reader doesn't understand the words you use, the crucial goal, which is communication, has not transpired. Or worse so far, they'll guess at the meaning and be wrong. Either way communication isn't happening. Moreover, if you have worldwide customers, American English is not possibly their first language, so colloquial or slang terms may not be understood or could be misinterpreted.

Meanwhile face to face communication isn't always possible, avoid thinking of yourself as 'hiding' behind an email; instead, consider about how you're being 'revealed' through an email. Email inspires people to express thoughts they wouldn't voice out in person and at times we do not review our messages as cautiously as we should before sending. So that what may be 'revealed' is a inconsiderate, careless person and except that's your goal, you might want to review your message a little more carefully. Think about how you would feel if the message was sent to you. Tone reflects your emotion, personality and intent what you want to reveal about yourself.

Sentence Arrangement

Intricate sentences, even if grammatically precise, may hide your significance. Emails are normally read quickly and merely once, so deliver brief and precise sentences. Your reader should not read through your email and deliberate on what you are trying to say, if it's a marketing email, it will be removed without a second look.

Concealing the Message

The starting of an email message can instantly set the tone and emphasizes the content of a message. Being vague or indirect won't get you what you want in an email. Set a direct tone by relating the most important info first, even if the major point of the message is bad news; do not bury it in the middle like it's not important or where it might be ignored.

Bold/Caps

This error is made often; but, if you send your text in all caps and bolded you'll just make your reader mad. Several times we have to send emails when we're angry, but try to stay balanced. Despite you're mad and want to scream, concentrate on what you want and often a more subtle technique can entice your anticipated results. LARGE SECTIONS OF TEXT IN ALL CAPS IS HARD TO READ. Again, communication is your goal, so make the font easy to read, let the content reveal to the reader your point, not your font.

Stylized Fonts

Meanwhile communication is the aim, if your reader can't read your font, there's no communication. When you send a message that you want to be taken seriously in curlicue, silly font, how can it be taken seriously? Keep fanciful fonts with whimsical messages and casual fonts with people you know casually. Normally, stick to Arial or New Times Roman, so the font doesn't distract your message.

Editing Software

Always spell and check your grammars properly. If you're in sales or marketing, when dealing with delicate material or sending emails to meticulous recipients you may want to consider using a software editor. A program like Grammar Expert Plus or Serenity's Editor can perform checks further than what a spell/grammar check can do, like tell the dissimilarity between 'in to' and 'into' or between 'form' and 'from.' Moreover, these programs can offer word suggestions to assist you change or stylize the tone of your message. If your writing is regarded as careless, customers may think you're careless in other ways as well. While slumping back in our chair and poking fun at our friends might be welcomed and suitable behavior at a casual dinner party, it's not going to get you what you want in an essential email. We're all familiar with the attitude and attire needed to deliver an efficient proposal, but rush over our electronic correspondence; the email. Only because emails are quick, doesn't mean they should necessarily be written quickly, sending a poorly written email sets a bad tone. Tone in written language is almost like body language, it goes beyond grammar and language and projects attitude. So before you click 'send,' reason about your objective and whether the tone used is going to help you or prevent you from getting what you want.

HOW TO CHOOSE THE NARRATOR

We've had the chance to work with some extraordinarily experienced and talented editors at Reedsy. Kristen Stieffel is amongst them: a writer, writing coach and editor, she specializes in hypothetical fiction. Today, she gives her expert advice on narrators and viewpoint. Ever questioned if you should write your book using first or third person? Well, you need to read this! Viewpoint, also regarded to as point of view or POV, is among the most complex aspects of fiction. It's confusing and misinterpreted, that's what makes viewpoint error among the most common errors editors comprehend in new writers' manuscripts. Misunderstanding about viewpoint stems from the actual words we use to define it: "close third person, limited third person and middle third person". What do they mean? 'Third person' does not say anything about viewpoint. It only says you are using he and she instead of I.

"Viewpoint isn't about pronouns. Viewpoint is about character."

Consider of viewpoint as a camera. Who is carrying it? You have two choices: it's either you give it to a narrator, or give it to one or more characters.

The omniscient narrator

The omniscient narrator understands everything and can share anyone's thoughts at all time. He can, and sometimes does, make value judgments towards the characters in the story.Even though most of the concentration in this story is on

Scrooge, he doesn't hold the viewpoint. The omniscient narrator does. The narrator makes verdicts, calling Scrooge a "squeezing, wrenching, grasping, scraping, covetous, clutching, old sinner". The narrator has a voice and behavior of his own. Scrooge would not even get that joke about houses playing hide-and-seek, let alone tell it. When we rephrased this passage from his viewpoint, it would change severely, making different remarks and judgments and no jokes at all.

The limited narrator

The limited narrator can share the thoughts of a selected few characters, usually only one per scene. He seldom makes value judgments. He can take a long view, or focus on a single character. Follett's narrative voice is not that of the boys. 'First footprints to blemish its perfect surface' is not a phrase these rapscallions would think of. We can tell the viewpoint is with the narrator, because it sees the boys collectively. If the viewpoint were with any one of them, the scene would be completely different, and the narrative would have that boy's voice. Limited narrator viewpoint is often mistaken for character viewpoint because both are usually written in the third person. The difference is in whether the narrative voice is distinct from the character's voice. We'll discuss this more when we get to character viewpoint.

The objective narrator

The objective narrator is like a photojournalist. He reports the story events, but he doesn't judge and doesn't read minds. The narrator's camera is mounted in the room, so we see and hear what's going on, but we don't know what the characters are thinking. Just as if we were waiting in the train station with this couple, all we can know is what we see and hear. If this scene were written from the viewpoint of either character, we would know that person's thoughts. Revealing the thoughts of either one would reveal too much, so Hemingway chooses the impartial objective narrator. This style of narrator is also useful if the writer needs to show something happening— a volcano erupting, a bomb ticking, an asteroid hurtling through space—when no person is there to observe it. Any narrator may hold the camera. But only the omniscient and limited narrators provide commentary, though to differing degrees. The objective narrator is a silent observer, with an unremarkable, almost invisible, prose style. In omniscient viewpoint, and to a lesser extent in limited viewpoint, it's possible for the narrator to have a distinct personality. I would go so far as to say that in omniscient viewpoint, it is necessary that the narrator persona have a distinct personality, like the narrator of A Christmas Carol.

The drawback to all of these is that any narrator puts psychic distance between the reader and the character. The advantage is that you can reveal information not known to the characters, or known to one character but not another. The narrator of A Christmas Carol, for example, tells the reader what other people think of Scrooge—things he cannot know. Remember that your protagonist is not the viewpoint character. He is not carrying the camera. Your narrator holds the camera, but he's not a character in the story. He is a persona observing the story. Next time we'll look at what it means to give the viewpoint completely to the characters.

HOW TO ESTABLISH SETTINGS

Setting is that aspect of your novel that gives the readers a sense of place and time. Read Elizabeth Chadwick's novels and you'll see she does a wonderful job of putting her readers in the center of a medieval faire, complete with banners, knights, lords and ladies. You'll almost hear the rumblings of carts over cobblestones. David L. Robbins jams his readers into the center of a gory World War II battlefield where you can just about feel the heat of the bullet as it zips by your head. How is it these and other authors are so adept at placing their readers in the middle of their novels?

They have mastered the art of setting.

Setting can be one of the most enjoyable aspects of novel writing. Think of it like this. You get to control the weather, the landscape and even what people wear. Now ain't that fun? When you learn to effectively construct setting in your writing, you have developed the ability to bring to life not only your characters but the very ground upon which they walk.

So, how does one go about developing a believable setting?

Let's consider how it should be used. Author Joanne Reid says, "Setting should be like good wallpaper. It enhances your story, fits perfectly, and does not overwhelm the people in the room." With that in mind, let's introduce several aspects to setting which you create to give your readers a full sense of time and place. They are:

- The geographical location of your story

- The time in which your story takes place

- The climate and/or weather in your story

- The lifestyle of your characters

5. The atmosphere or emotional quality of your story

The geographical location of your novel is wherever you wish it or whatever is necessary to the story. It helps if you are able to write about a place you know, but it's often more interesting if you create your own world as a backdrop to your manuscript. It is important your setting is as authentic as you can make it for readers can spot a mistake in less time than it took to write it. The time in which your story takes place is again, whatever you wish or need to tell your tale. The type of story you craft will often dictate the time. The secret is to learn, or imagine as the case may be, as much about the era in which you write. In my case, I write about people involved in the American Civil War. Therefore, I walk the battlefields on which my stories will take place. I study the land, the roads, the natural defensive positions, locations of fences and the like. I seek out those towns with structures that date to the mid-nineteenth century and even photograph them, so as to better understand their architectural aspects. I visit museums where uniforms, dresses and even quilts of the time are exhibited. Then, as I write, all these things assist me in creating a true to life setting for my readers.

Climate is one of my favorite aspects to setting, though many writers forget to use it to its maximum advantage. To me, it offers so much in the way of establishing the mood of a scene. It also gives a writer any number of opportunities to incorporate sound and visual enhancements to their story. Lifestyle is the day-to-day experiences of your characters. This is an aspect to setting that generally comes out in the story of its own volition. However, the best writers specifically use this as a tool in constructing setting. Atmosphere is the mood or feeling of your book. It offers your reader the emotional quality of your story. As with all aspects of setting, it can change as the novel progresses.

How do you introduce setting to your readers?

As with any part of your novel, stay clear of info dumps. Bring your setting to the forefront by using all the tools available to you. Employ dialogue, narration, character actions, speech patterns and so on. Be cautious, however, of establishing your setting by lengthy narration for you never want to sound like a travel guide.

ESTABLISHING THE SETTING

To advance the plot or enhance conflict

Think of how the setting might disrupt the plans of your antagonist or protagonist. Say your major character is being hunted by an assassin. How might an eclipse allow your hero to escape his intended murder? If your novel is based on a historical battle, how might rolling hills, like those on the Gettysburg Battlefield, influence the outcome?

Setting Creates Consistency within Plots and Subplots.

Your novel will have its plot points and subplots with delicate threads woven through the pages. A consistent setting can keep it all joined together so the reader mentally stays within a comfortable framework.

Use Setting to Enhance Conflict.

Think about a scene with rumbling thunder and stabs of lightning in the inky sky. Does that create more tension, whatever the scene, than say an idyllic spring day in the park? Should you wish to use that tranquil day among the flowers, how about plopping a flock of buzzards in the middle of that field. You think your reader would have a heightened sense of mood as the birds begin to circle overhead?

Use it to illustrate a Character's Character.

The manner in which your characters speak, dress, move and curse will evoke in your reader a picture of this person. Imagine a dockhand who never utters a profane word. Would that image provide an insight into your character? What if your hero, Paul, always dressed in plaid and carried an ax? Would that be enough to exhibit his character or would he still need a blue ox to complete the picture? Before I close, I'd like to offer you one last tip as to setting. Employ your readers' five senses. All authors seem to work in sight and sound by rote, but many aspiring writers miss the other three senses. Ensure your characters also smell, taste and feel their surroundings and your readers will do the same.

HOW TO DEVELOP WELL DRAWN CHARACTERS

Protagonist

So I have talked about a couple types of protagonists, and how to make them: Antiheroes and horse. As well as what types of Character to

Use or to stay away from. But not all Protagonists will be an antihero or hero. Today, I am going to talk about what universal attributes make a great protagonist, which will take your story forward. Keep in mind, the key to all of these steps must be written down, so feel free to take a notebook, or format and print the page so that you can fill them out like a worksheet.

Create a list of all the attributes and ideas you have for your Protagonist: Yes, I recognize that you already have a protagonist in mind, prepared to go and boot some butt. But before you put in your protagonist into the world, you have to make sure that they are prepared. Writing their attributes down is a magnificent way to set off your brain into feeling protected; so that it is not busy trying to memorize all of your protagonist's attributes, and can concentrate on perfecting them.

Identify the part of yourself that the Protagonist is coming from: Every character you make is a part of you; especially the protagonist. That is not to say that any of them should be a direct copy of you, but a little piece of your past, imagination, or personality. Even characters that don't embody your real attributes embody those that you either fear becoming, wish you were, or hate. Figure out, and write down on your note, what component of you this character is drawing its creative energy from; how you bond to this character.

List the differences between yourself and your Protagonist: List the psychological, personality, and behavioral differences between your character and you. Why? Because this will definitely help you put solid meaning to your protagonist; like the tracing of a drawing. It also helps you to witness your protagonist as part of the story; more than as an addition of you. This is important for being able to get the distance required to edit and refine your protagonist, and to breathe a life of their own into them, that your audience will definitely notice.

Identify what your Protagonist wants and how badly they want it: As we have discussed before, your story must be driven by your characters. As such, you have to figure out what is inspiring your protagonist to progress forward and to do lot thing that will comprise the story itself. This way, every time your protagonist comes with contact with an obstacle, you can judge immediately how they respond, based on whether their actions will guide them to their goal, and if they are worth the effort. What is necessary to achieve their goal? Just make sure that their flaws make sense and are deeply rooted in the core of the protagonist's character, and are not clichés or pseudo-flaws that you threw in just to complete the checklist.

Figure out how the Protagonist can develop, using the Three-Act Story Outline: Fill out Three-Act Outline (and perhaps read why an Outline is so vital), because we will be making using of the Holy Crap out of that baby; including here. A good story will be directly connected to the destruction or growth of the protagonist's character. Use your outline, go to every plot-point and figure out how they will add to the growth or destruction of your protagonist; how the story events will affect their flaws, and improve their character. Put thoughts is parentheses by each plot-point, and be prepared to adjust them if and when the need arises.

Fill out a Character Attribute Sheet: I am not going to tell you which one (although I may create one eventually), because how much character facts you want to have prepared before the story starts, is completely up to you. Large Character Sheets have the profit of great specificity, but are frequently so long and tedious as to misplace writers in boredom, and do not allow them know more about their character over the course of writing the story. Regardless, I commend filling out a little one, at least, and gazing over a long one, just to give you new thoughts for character facts and to help you notice any basic or advanced points you may have forgotten to enhance to your protagonist's description.

Antagonist

In simple terms, the antagonist is the character which a story has, a novel or in a literary work that makes resistance or hostility; often towards your major character (protagonist). He or she is usually adversarial but not necessarily or is competing with another character. It is this character that lets the story to achieve excitement, make fun and also make a page turner for your reader.

How do I develop an antagonist character?: An antagonist character can come from any foundation. Much alike the protagonist in a story, this character can be advanced as a result of someone known to you, family, friends, strangers or acquaintances. The antagonist character come from people at your work place or can even be acquaintances developed from drawing into your own experiences. The impression behind the antagonist is to block or impede your major character from reaching his/her goal. In some cases the antagonist is a villain and immoral but not always. Antagonists are various times depicted in a negative method but sometimes they could be funny characters. You can make humor showing your antagonist resisting your major character.

Just as the protagonist, your antagonist must also have a goal. The same rules are applied. The goal can be at the top, it can be pointless, it can be violent or it can be foolish but remember to make a goal that will be in conflict with your major character. Usually the excellent stories come together when the antagonist is in straight conflict with the protagonist. It is significant for your antagonist to have an inspiration. Clearly know and define the inspiration. It can be that your antagonist is angry, jealous, has a compulsion, and is simply wants power or greedy. Whichever one you chose you need to guarantee that one exists.

In addition, make certain sure that your antagonist has a fighting chance above your protagonist. It makes the story more acceptable and interesting. It is just as important way to understand and improve your antagonist's fighting means to help carry the story through. Just as your protagonist, your antagonist must have more than one dimension. Nobody likes to read about a narrow character. The more dimensions you provide your characters the better your story will read. The major point is to block the protagonist's progress. It does not have to be immoral or crazy or frightening but it should block the goal or progress in a way. As with your protagonist, try to make your antagonist interesting. Making an emotional connection with your character. The emotional connection for the reader will most likely be a dislike to your antagonist. Also, recall making the antagonist's goals realistic as the antagonist can gain over your protagonist.

It's important to show your antagonist's modus operandi. This means that you need to display how your character operates in life. You must guarantee that logic follows through for your character. What creates him 'tick' or how does he solve situations? Is he always a undesirable person? Does he always breakdown the rules or is it just when it comes to the protagonist? These are all the things that need to be well-defined for your antagonist to make him/her real. This will allow your reader to become invested in the story. Your antagonist's character can improve throughout the story just as your protagonist but try making sure you know whcre that development is heading to.

Minor/Supporting

We write a more about major characters here at MW, and, of course, we devote a good deal of time discussing rascals as well. And there are also good reasons for doing both. A compelling, believable protagonist can carry a story a long way. There are little things more fun in literature than an actual frightening and evil villain. Today, though, I would like to move attention away from the stars of our books to the secondary characters, the people who devote as much time in the background of our books as they do in the limelight. While the protagonists and rascals may drive the narrative, it is frequently the secondary characters that are most unforgotten.

Unfortunately, while reading a novel, there are also times when, I will find that the major characters have been crafted with caution, but the secondary characters are level, like cardboard cutouts. Just as well-drawn minor characters can enhance a novel, poorly drawn ones can sap the energy out of our narrative and ruin an otherwise brilliant story. I have written before about the things I did to build my characters. I would not bother with all those facts again, but I would need you to go back and read the post I have linked to on the ABCs of

Character Improvement. Because the first key in creating good minor characters is to devote as much time and energy drawing them, developed their trait, their motivation, their backgrounds, as we do working on our major characters. There are no shortcuts to good character improvement. It takes time, it takes work. The payout for that work, though, is a constellation of stars in our work instead of just one or two. Do the major characters matter more? I suppose the answer is yes, in an absolute sense. They're in almost every scene. If they are our POV characters, then their voices are important to the success of our books. It is easy to determine that their development is most significant. But there is alternative another way to look at this: every character is the star or co-star of whatever scene he/she is in. For that second in the narrative when any certainly give character appears, he/she will be the focus of our readers' attention. And meanwhile we do not want our narrative to flag at any point in the book, meanwhile we want to keep our readers involved at all times, we cannot afford to let any character look flat or poorly drawn. Again, this may seem basic, but you would be amazed by the number of writers who do not give all of their characters the attention they earn and need.

To escape this, I frequently like to take the idea of giving a cautious attention to my secondary characters a step to promote. I hope that my major characters; my hero and villain; will be unforgettable on their own terms. Their roles in the plotting of my books nearly guarantee that this is so. But in order to create those minor characters shine a little bit more brightly, I like to take chances with them. I might make them particularly quirky; offering to them unusual ways or speaking, or uncommon physical traits. I might hide something in their backgrounds or in their current circumstances that will guarantee that they play a crucial role in the resolution of my central conflict. There are no restrict to what I can do with them; the very fact that they are minor characters provides me the freedom to challenge myself, to do something truly unusual. And, as you might expect, that makes them especially fun to play with.

The other thing I like to do with my minor characters, particularly in my multi-thread, multi-POV epic fantasy work, is use them as point of view characters. Why? A couple of reasons. First, I believe it can be effective occasionally not too often to see my main characters through the eyes of other people. This gives my reader a different perspective on those key characters, and it gives some variety to the voices telling my story. Second, relying on what those minor characters do for a living, what role they play in my world and my plot, telling a piece of the story through their eyes which give my readers a new and unique perspective on my world building, and on the twists and turns of my narrative.

All of us have come in contact those memorable minor characters in our reading. Neville Long bottom and Luna Love good in the Harry Potter books; Bean in ENDER'S GAME; Gurney Halleck and Duncan Idaho in Dune. As readers, we know how much that can added to a book or series. As writers, we should place that knowledge to work. We should take the additional time to increase those characters, to make them as real, as exciting, as sympathetic as the major characters to whom we give so much time and effort.

So, who are some of your preferred minor characters from books you are read? And what do you do to make your minor characters position out? Conflict is at the heart of every novel; so much so that the portion revolves around the 'core' conflict. Without conflict to force a portion, scenes fall flat, not succeed to hook readers, and go nowhere. But conflict is not always about fighting or putting the protagonist face to face with the antagonist. It is just two things that occur to be at odds with each other. You want to go swimming, but you do not want to get wet. You want to tell your best friend some secret, but you know she is a horrible gossip. You want that brand new car, but you need to pay rent. Something is in the method of what you want and that problem has to be resolved before having it. Because of the selection of conflicts available, introducing conflict in your novel is easier than it looks. Simply put a hindrance in the way of what your protagonist wishes to accomplish, either on a physical or an emotional level.

HOW TO CREATE CONFLICT

Force a character to face a fear

The man scared of heights is not going to want to crawl out on a ledge for anything. Putting the thing he needs most out on that ledge forces him to do just that Janice Hardy or he fails. Consider what your protagonist is scared of and what he might never, ever, do if it involved that fear. Then look for ways to make him do it.

Offer an impossible choice

Choices move the plot, but not possible choices make the protagonist work for it. When there's no plain answer, and both choices have awful consequences, readers know a bit about the story is going to change and the stakes are going up; two solid ways to keep readers hooked. How may you force your protagonist to make an impossible choice?

Make someone go against their beliefs

We all have lines we vow we will never cross, but what happens when there is no other choice? The pacifist who has to resort to fighting to get what he needs or the husband who puts his wife at danger for personal gains. Look for places where you can check your protagonist's beliefs, and where they may fail those beliefs.

Keep secrets

Uncertainty and distrust can make a character second guess everything he/she does, which can lead to bad judgment and mistakes. Even more entertainment, is a character who has a secret and is actively working against the protagonist; even if nobody but the author knows it. Think about what your protagonist does not know or who might be holding back helpful info.

Have bad days

Ever had one of those days when you thought the universe was going after you? Characters have those days, too. Red lights when the protagonist is in a rush, small annoyances that pile up, tiny things that cause large blowups later. The small problems are not always what cause the conflict, but they disturb the protagonist's emotional state and that creates this work. Being in a bad mood or at the beginning of your patience means an impaired decision-making process. Look for way to heap small annoyances onto your protagonist so when she wants a clear head to make a critical conclusion, she does not have one.

Allow disagreements

A close friend who thinks the protagonist's ideal is a bad idea provides just as enough conflict as a showdown with the antagonist (more actually, because this one is more personal). Conflict can come from enemies as well as friends, because not everyone will blindly agree to what your protagonist needs to do. Give your secondary characters their own tough opinions and let them butt heads with the protagonist.

Get emotional

The more individual something is, the tougher it can be to walk away and let it go. Striking a character's emotional hot buttons can transform a mild debate into a marriage-ending fight. An added bonus, the more individual the obstacle in the protagonist's way, the more possible the reader will care about the conclusion of that struggle. Consider how you might deepen any individual connection your protagonist has to your goals and hindrances in your scenes. Conflicts keeps your portion moving, and the extra varied you make them, the more unpredictable the story will be, an unpredictable plot will make readers guessing, eager to know what would be happening next.

INTERNAL AND EXTERNAL CONFLICT

External conflict used to be the primary form of conflict in genre or common fiction. Only in extra literary works did heroes develop, change, or even question themselves much. Your genre fiction protagonist knew he/she was a better person than the villain and had no purpose to change. So the pressure in the story was all about whether the hero may outfight or outwit the villain at the climax, which made for shallow characterization. However, even writers of children's cartoons and book put more emotional depth in the children stories by giving their main characters internal conflict as well as outer conflict. Here's a simple way to differentiate between the two in terms of Dramatical theory. The best way to understand outer conflict is that it relays to the Story Goal. Dramatical sees every story as an effort to resolve a problem or accomplish a goal. The Story Goal is the product being sought.

While some of the characters in your story will be affected by this effort in some way , the main outer conflict will be between two characters. Your Protagonist will be the key character who pursues the Story Goal and the person whose choice determines the outcome. Your Antagonist will be the character conflicted to the Story Goal, who wants the Protagonist to fail, and who ensures everything in his/her power to assured the Goal is not attained. In high school literature classes, we were taught that outer conflict came in several selections:

- To be politically correct Person vs. Person

- Person vs. Society

- Person vs. Nature

- Person vs. Machine

- Person vs. demons

However, we can shorten this and say your Antagonist can be dressed up in any guise as a person, animal, institution, monster, machine, force of nature, society, abstract idea, etc. All what matters is that he/she/ can effectively oppose the Protagonist's effort to accomplished the goal.

Internal Conflict: Internal conflict concerns your key character's self-doubt – his/her dilemma over the best way to accomplish the Story Goal. All of us have been in conditioned where we were outside our luxury zone, where we were uncertain if our way of behaving is the correct way to accomplish our goals. For instance, suppose you devote several years at university being the life of the party and hanging out with very laid-back, arts major, unpretentious. Then one day, you have your first job interview a big company. This prospect leads to certain internal conflict.

How would you present yourself at the interview? Would you change your personality and unpretentious to look like someone who would fit in with the corporate world? Would you buy a suit and some real shoes, get a nice haircut, etc.? Is it time to drop swear words and colloquial language from your vocabulary? Or maybe you should lose your cynicism about the corporate world and start gushing enthusiasm and optimism? On the other hand, you may decide to stick to who you are. After all, you have had success with your approach in other endeavors. You get along well with people. The interviewers may value honesty over pretension. Maybe this company has a calmer atmosphere that rewards individuality and creativity more than conformity? Or maybe you would find more happiness working for a company that better fits your beliefs?

Either way, no matter how well you research the company forward of time, you still would not certainly the right way to present yourself until you truly get a job offer. In this scenario, the external conflict is you vs. all the other applicants competing for the job. The internal conflict would be dilemma over the best way to present you at the interview. Readers relay to characters that have internal conflicts as well as external conflicts. More outstandingly, your major character's internal conflict creates suspense, because readers won't know how he will resolve his personal dilemma until the moment of crisis. Will your major character make the right decision? What is the right decision? These questions keep your readers interested in the story.

CHAPTER 3:
ADVANCED TIPS FOR THAT CREATIVE EDGE

A Creative writing is any form of writing which is already written with the creativity of mind: poetry writing, fiction writing, creative nonfiction writing etc. The purpose is to define something, whether it be thoughts, feelings, or emotions. Rather than simply giving info or inciting the reader to make an action beneficial to the writer, creative writing is written to entertain or educate someone, to spread awareness about something or someone, or to simply express one's thoughts. But there are two types of creative writing: good and bad. Bad creative writing can't make any impression on the reader. You do not want to do that, do you? Of course not. So whether you are a poet, a novelist, a short-story writer, an essayist, a biographer or just an aspiring beginner, you will want to perfect your craft. But the question is: how? When writing great poetry, nonfiction, or fiction, amazing things can happen. Readers cannot put it down. The work wrote by you becomes a bestseller. It becomes famous. But you have to get to that level... first. The best way to improve your proficiency in creative writing is to write, write compulsively, but it does not just mean write whatever you want. There are certain things you must know first... it helps to start with the right foot.

THE POWER OF DISCOVERY: DON'T ALWAYS WRITE ONLY WHAT YOU KNOW

Everyone at some point has read a story involving a prince, princess, or some kind of mythical creature. Now since you are here you are probably wondering how to create some of the magic of those stories. Well follow these steps and you will be well on your way to fighting your dragons with the help of a magic sword. So you have decided to write a creative story. Well that can mean anything from realistic to super fiction. So the first step is to choose what your overall theme is for your story: Fairytale, Bravery (of a knight or other person), Romance, Realistic situation in life, Or some other theme just make sure it is broad at this point.

Choose your characters: The best method to do this is to have a separate paper and write down their names, what they are and what they look like. It is also to determine things like what their personalities are like here too so when you are writing you can think of what they would do. In detail I personally have an 'interview' of my character. Create random situations and see how they would respond to them.

So now you have characters: determine where they should be put. Yes it is time for the setting. Do you want them to live in a abandoned wood. Maybe they live in a crazy, busy city? It will affect how you write because you will want to describe the places they are and what they will be wearing.

Write the plot. What are these character's purposes? What are the main events? What is going to happen in the story? Think of this like a road-map so on days when you have writers block you can go back to this plot chart and go yeah I will write about that!

Put it all together and include all the facts. Remember the more facts the easier it is to picture. Also remember to include tons of chatter between your characters. It is a good impression to have fights and romantic moments between your characters. This makes the story more acceptable so that people feel like fiction might not be quite so, well fiction.

Now go out there and get your magic pen out and write up the next Harry Potter story!

HOW TO WORK

TIME MANAGEMENT AND HANDLING DEADLINES

Time management is suitable for anyone who wants to complete a writing project in a thorough way. To-do lists, planning, prioritizing, and organization all play a part in the productive use of time. One of the advantages of successful time supervision is avoiding the circumstance of rushing to get a task finished or a work project completed. In a stressful business environment, a web based appointment scheduler helps you minimize time finished on scheduling. Time management practices can prove useful to someone who needs a little more organization when it comes to his/her work and the scheduling of appointments.

Creating To-Do Lists

- A to-do list can include fun activities. In fact, writing down a leisure activity on a to-do list is a great way of making sure that relaxation time is incorporated into a day.

- A to-do list is a simple tool to employ when it comes to organizing a day's work.

- A to-do list must be flexible. For instance, sometimes deadlines for projects are moved up creating the need to move items around on the to-do list.

- Check off or put a line through each task when it is completed. This illustrates a person's progress throughout the day.

- Each day write a list of things to be accomplished beginning with high priority tasks.

Setting Priorities

- The arrival of an unexpected assignment means that the day's work priorities will likely need to be adjusted in order finish items on schedule.

- Setting priorities is a great way to organize work hours as well as make the most productive use of them.

- In setting priorities for the day, take the time to decide which tasks need to be completed right away.

- If a person is assigned a time-consuming project, they may want to break the work up into manageable portions to be worked on over time.

- A person should review all of the tasks that they need to complete, in order to decide how much time to dedicate to each one.

Meeting Deadlines

- If a person writes down project deadlines as well as keeps them on hand, he or she will always know what work needs to be completed and when.

- When it comes to meeting a project deadline, planning a time schedule to complete the work is essential.

- A person should endeavor to finish a project before its deadline in order to have some extra time for last minute changes.

- A person who meets project deadlines is demonstrating professionalism to clients, bosses, and coworkers around them.

- Before jumping into a work project, a person would be wise to review all aspects of it. An overall understanding of the project will give the person some insight on how much work time to set aside for it.

Setting Goals and Achieving Them

- Setting goals can help a person learn how to better organize their time. For instance, setting a goal to finish a project two days before its deadline teaches a person to use their work time effectively.

- Setting goals and then writing them down is an effective way for a person to focus his or her efforts.

- Setting a goal and achieving it lends confidence to a person in all areas of their work.

- Once a goal is achieved, it usually inspires a person to set a higher goal, which improves work performance.

Organize and Develop a Daily Routine

- When making a decision on how to spend time a person should consider the level of importance of the task or project.

- When facing a heavy workload, a daily routine can help with organization.

- When a person develops a daily routine, it helps to balance the amount of time that is dedicated to each task or work project.

- Make Decisions More Efficiently: Don't Procrastinate.

- Endlessly putting off a decision is stressful to a person. It's a better idea to think something over for a reasonable amount of time and then make a decision.

- An important part of time management is deciding how to spend one's time. In other words, a person shouldn't try to accomplish everything in one day, but instead choose a few things to focus on.

- A written daily schedule can help to focus a person's efforts on one task at a time.

- A daily routine must sometimes be adjusted to allow for unexpected occurrences or projects that consume more time than expected.

CHAPTER 4:
READY, SET, GOAL: SHIFT YOUR MINDSET INTO GEAR!

Got an idea that you just cannot shake? That idea could manifest itself as a book or a business. I've spent a lot of time talking about how entrepreneurs should approach a new business and I've found out that there are a lot more parallels between starting up a business and launching a new book than you could imagine. As I launch my first book, 'The Entrepreneur Equation', paradoxically on launching businesses, I believed I would share a few insights on the relationship between the two.

What's Your Aim?

Deciding to start a business is different from deciding to start a successful business. The tactics to open one store vs. a goal of creating a large nationwide retail chain vary significantly. It's hard to know what steps to take if you do not know your end goal. The same goes for your book. What is your end game? Are you consuming it as a calling card to get more clients? Are you looking for a label of achievement like "best seller status" for your brand? Are you planning to make gobs of money from it or are you using it to blowout a message (by the way, if your aim is to make gobs of money, you may want to chat with a few industry professionals first). These goals will expressively impact the strategy and planning of not only your manuscript, but the launching and marketing of your book. And while you are at it, you might as well set the biggest objective that you can. Nothing happens if you do not achieve your stretch goal, but as Wayne Gretzky says, "You miss 100% of shots that you never take"

Understand Your Customer

It's always crucial to understand your clients. To be successful in writing, you've to know what pain point you are solving for your customer and how you are delivering value. Plus, if "everyone" is your customer, you're going to have a hard time reaching anyone at all, so having a focus is critical. The same goes for your book (particularly non-fiction books). Ask yourself what solid benefits your readers will take away from investing their time and money into your book. Who's your specific reader and what qualitative and quantitative benefits are they after? This will shape not only how you deliver your message in the book, but also how you plan to advertise your book.

The Idea Isn't Valued; It is The Execution

In an era where we have access to essentially everything we want and need, including a whole bunch of crap we do not care about, it's hard to have a true novel idea (joke intended). Having the idea for a business is not appreciated; it's executing on the business plan every day. The same goes for a book. Once you have the idea, you've to write the manuscript and then market it. A lot of publishers care at least as much, if not more, about your marketing plan than the content of the book. So, even if you have a fabulous idea, if you can't or do not want to pound the pavement to meet your goals, there is not a lot of value there.

The Day You 'Open For Business' Is Where The Hard Work Begins.

Considering a business idea and writing your plan is a cakewalk compared to what you've to bear day in and day out to make your business successful. The same goes for a book. The most common mistake is that you're done when you finish writing- totally wrong. Writing the manuscript, as dreadful as it may seem, is trivial compared to everything that comes after. Prepare to devote much time and effort after the book has been written. The takeaway: Make sure you assess and prepare for launching a book, just as you would do in a business, if you want to be successful with it.

LUCRATIVE BOOK WRITING

There are over 11,000 business books published every year in the US. And that does not include self-published print or eBooks; of which there are tens of thousands, growing exponentially every year. And yet, I suggest that writing a book; a good book, mind be incredibly helpful to you and to your business. Let us start by defining our terms. By "good book" I mean one that's well-written (grammatically and syntactically correct, with complete sentences and appropriate ,understandable vocabulary); consist of clearly stated, useful ideas; and it's engaging; meaning readers will be drawn in and fascinated or bored and confused. So, assuming you have written such a book, how will that help you or your business? In 2006, Mike Schultz, principal of the Wellesley Hills Group, of Framingham, Mass., strong-willed to find out. His firm, a marketing consultancy for expert service providers, gave out the results of a survey of 200 business-book authors. They refer to it as The Business impact of writing a Book. In an article on BusinessWeek that same year, Schulz said

"The vast majority of the authors we surveyed — 96% — said they did realize an important positive impact on their businesses from writing a book and would suggest the practice. He continues to note, though, that the primary business benefits are not direct; that's, even the authors whose books sold well did not make much money from the sales of books. The gains they cited were things like "generating more leads, closing more deals, charging higher fees, and getting better speaking engagements. I have certainly seen those results in my own business; I have other friends and colleagues who have written business books. Here is why I think those things happen when you write a good business book:

Personal integrity: Having a book published cause people to think you are smarter and more expert. I do not know if you get the same result through self-publishing, but it is definitely been true in my experience of having books published with traditional publishers. As soon as my first book came out, at the end of 2006, you'd think by the way others responded to me that I would suddenly gain 20 IQ points. It was almost disorienting – I knew I was the same person, but formerly closed doors magically opened, and people I knew would not have paid much attention to what I said before were suddenly listening carefully. It was enormously helpful in creating initial connections with potential customers and business partners.

Business credibility: If you are running a business and you publish a good book, your business gets a radiance effect from your rise in credibility. Being associated with a business book and its author gives enterprise legitimacy in the eyes of the world. Being rendered more legitimate simply makes it easier to get things done. In my experience, it also gives a lift to everyone who works in the organization – it becomes a source of self-importance and espirit de corps.

Brand clarity: Having a book or books that lay out the key academic property or the core models or ethics of your business really helps potential customers understand what you are about and how you can be of value to them. It can also help your own staff be clearer about who you're and what you are offering. People have often been astonished when I have said this – they question whether it is really a good idea to put your ideas out for the public to see (and, by implication, steal). But our experience has been that the ideas in a book quite regularly whet people's appetite for more in-depth knowledge or consulting.

Having noted all these powerful benefits – and the positive outcomes that they can bring, "let me add a note of caution." Schulz also noted: It may sound cleat, but the biggest finding was that authors who sold more than 10,000 copies of their books were much more satisfied with how the effort paid off than those who sold fewer than 10,000. Those who sold 20,000 copies or higher were off the chart in their enthusiasm. So, more than anything else we measured, the number of books sold was the biggest factor contributing to the project's success. We also found out that people who self-published, did not use a actual agent or hire a PR firm, and did not do a lot of public speaking, sold fewer books and were much less pleased with the process. So, if you have a book in you, writing it might help you and your business in a host of ways. However, writing it is just the beginning. Then you have to concentrate on selling it: the more you do that, the more you will see a return on your investment.

CHAPTER 5:
START WRITING

Writing a book is one of the most challenging and rewarding things you will ever do. We won't sugarcoat it: it takes serious determination, patience and hard work to finish a book. Talent? That's not nearly as important as you think. In fact, with courses like this, you can write a book in just 30 days. Every writer develops her own way of writing a book. Some like to pump out hundreds of pages of rough drafts, others deliberate over each and every word put to paper. As you develop a taste for writing, you will soon discover a method that works for you. But for absolute beginners, this blog post should serve as a good starting point.

Pick a Genre

Take a quick glance at your bookshelf. What do you see? Picking a genre is the first step in writing a book. Don't base this choice on what genres sell best, but what you like to read. A hardcore sci-fi fan writing a 'new adult' novel is only going to produce a shoddy book – if she finishes it at all. In other words, write for yourself, not the market. Stephen King puts it best: "When you write a story, you're telling yourself the story. When you rewrite, your main job is taking out all the things that are not the story. Your stuff starts out being just for you, but then it goes out."

Start from the End

Endings are the hardest part of any story. Don't take our word for it; just ask any writer buddies of yours. Most beginners start out strong but find themselves flummoxed by the time the ending draws near. It doesn't help that the ending is also the thing that stays longest with readers. So before you put a single word to paper, figure out how your story ends. Not how it begins – that can be redrawn and revised indefinitely – how it closes. Work your way backwards. How does the character(s) reach his/her ultimate fate? What are the catalysts that lead to the close? What was their origin? And so on. Your plots will sound much more plausible and you'll avoid the dreaded Deus Ex Machine that plagues so much fiction. Want to write a book fast? Take this easy to follow course on writing and publishing books by Mindy Gibbins-Klein.

Create Your Characters

Characters, not plots, are the soul of good writing. You don't recall the story from Henry V;

you recall Falstaff. The plot of Catcher in the Rye is mostly superfluous. It's Holden Caulfield who holds your attention. Same with Sherlock Holmes, Atticus Finch, and Hercule Poirot. Characters stay with readers for generations, the stories are mostly forgotten. This is why you must draw out your characters before you start writing the book. These tips should help:

Write a Character Biography: When was the character born? What is her name? Who were her parents? Was she rich, poor, or middle-class? Where did she go to school? What did she study in college? Answering questions like these will help draw a deep portrait of the character and make her more convincing.

Understand the Character's Motivations: What does your character want? What are her motivations for doing what she does?

Understand Character Arc: Character arc refers to the character's development through the story. The essential quality of every good character is change. For example, Harry Potter starts off naïve and ends up a steely eyed adult, while Frodo Baggins is a nobody from Shire who ends up as the savior of Middle Earth.

Understand the Struggle: "Character A wants B, but C stands in the way". How A manages to overcome C and get B is the heart of any story. For example: Rocky wants to be a champion, but crushing poverty and Apollo Creed stand in his way. How he overcomes this is the meat of Rocky, not the final fight itself.

Make an Outline: Once you have your characters firmly in place, start creating an outline of the plot. This is meant to serve as a very rough guideline to hold the plot in place. You don't have to follow it word for word; feel free to improvise while you write.

Chiefly, the outline should:

- Give a brief overview of what happens in each chapter.

- Delineate the primary struggle in the novel.

- Show how different events and characters interact and affect each other (A murders B, C takes the fall, etc.)

- Allow plenty of room for improvisation

Write the First Draft: There is nothing to writing. All you do is sit down at a typewriter and bleed, The first draft is where you discover the story by yourself. As you write, you'll find characters and plots growing in directions you'd never thought possible. The outlines you wrote earlier will often be discarded as you experiment with characters, plots, styles and forms. This is a place for you to break the mold and push yourself creatively. Don't bother being perfect; the faster you can jot down ideas on paper, the better. Eventually, this rough collection of thoughts, ideas, and plotlines will come together into a comprehensible book – after due editing and countless revisions of course. For now, focus on writing – anything. Everyone has a book inside them. Learn how to write the book inside you with this course.

Get Yourself a Drink: Now that you're done with the first draft, head over to the nearest watering hole and grab yourself a drink. You've earned it.

Rewrite: This is the part where most writers fail. Slinging out a rough draft is easy enough; turning that incomprehensible mess into something readers would want to read takes time, patience and practice.

Ideally, you should give yourself a few months between first draft and first rewrite. This gives you the creative distance necessary to analyze the writing dispassionately. Ask sharp, pertinent questions – does the plot make sense? Are the characters convincible? Is the pace too slow? Too fast? Is the writing crisp and creative enough? Is the story fun to read? The first rewrite should take you considerably longer than the first draft. Don't worry about getting every word right – you'll take care of that during editing. For now, focus on pulling the rough ideas in the draft into a narrative that actually makes sense.

Edit:

Done with the first rewrite? Don't start partying yet. There is still lots of work to be done. Editing is the opposite of creative writing. Instead of spinning beautiful metaphors and creating lush imagery, you have to actually delete linguistic flourishes. The amazing adverb you found after an hour's search in the thesaurus? Gone. Those long-winded, poetic asides? Deleted.

To make this murder slightly easier, follow these tips:

Minimize Adverb Use: Adverbs are the lazy man's writing crutches. They reduce into a single word what should generally be conveyed by context. "He walked quickly to the door as Lily pulled into the garage" is not bad writing, it's lazy writing. Try being more descriptive – "He rushed to the door as soon as he heard Lily's car pull into the garage".

Use Plenty of Synonyms: This quote from Dead Poet's Society says it all:

"So avoid using the word 'very' because it's lazy. A man is not very tired, he is exhausted. Don't use very sad, use morose. Language was invented for one reason, boys – to woo women – and, in that endeavor, laziness will not do. It also won't do in your essays."

Tighten Up: A book is no place for lazy writing. Take out words and passages that aren't absolutely crucial to the story. Your book should be half its original length after a solid round of editing.

Get Outside Help: Most writers don't have the critical distance to edit their own books properly. Consider getting outside help – a professional editor or a friend – to look over your manuscript.

Congratulations – you've now written your very first book. This is the time to hit the clubs and party hard. Then wake up next morning and start working on your second book!

SECRETS OF BOOK WRITING

Anybody with a story to tell can write a book. Either for their own enjoyment or to publish for all to see. If you find yourself weaving creative narratives in your head as you read your favorite novels, or when you are relaxing in the park, consider writing your stories down. Although it may seem daunting, you can do it. We'll give you some pointers on how to get started. Also, take some time, sit around, and just think about what people like to read. Ask your friends and maybe you can come up with an amazing story!

Getting Started on Your Book

Buy a notebook: While you may or may not wish to type your novel directly into a computer, it's not always possible to be near one when inspiration strikes. Thus, it's best to have good old-fashioned pencil and paper no matter where you are. Moreover, many writers swear by the connection from mind to hand to pen on paper, so at least give it a go before dismissing this as an option to aid your writing experience. A leather-bound or heavy card notebook is the sturdiest and can take lots of abuse in a backpack or briefcase, whereas a spiral-bound notebook, while not as robust, is easy to keep open. Better still, should you decide the page you just wrote is utter garbage? Spiral or bound, consider using graph paper versus standard lined paper. You may end up creating drawings and sketches as you go, and it's useful for indenting paragraphs, or outlining.

Put your thinking cap on: Now that you have your notebook, it's time to squash the traditional bugaboo of all writers: that empty first page. Use those first pages to write out ideas for stories. Once you feel you've written down enough ideas, read over them. Twice. Then, take your ideas to someone else to get feedback. Decide which idea to go with and make sure it doesn't sound like anything recently published. Then, wait a few days, read over the idea again to be sure, and move onto the next step.

Create the overview of your story: including an outline, notes about places, all the little things that go into a larger story. There are several advantages to this overview approach, including: It will give you new ideas for your story as you describe different parts of it, Nothing goes to waste. You may describe a character, for instance, who never appears in the story directly but who influences another character.

Set up a table or chart and write down all the characters that have a special meaning in the story. Use your notebook to write a lot about them.—Even create a backstory for a couple of them. This helps you visualize and think about them more and even learn about your own character more. You always have something to refer to when you run out of immediate ideas.

Create your outline: An outline will help you define the arc of your narrative—the beginning, development of plot and characters, the setting up of all the events leading to the big conflict or climax, and then the resolution and ending. The beginning of the story is often the hardest part depending on who you are—if you want it to be. The best thing to do is start as broadly as possible. Say, for example, you want to write a mystery novel, and you're a fan of World War II. Write that down: Mystery, WWII. The beauty of this is that both categories are very broad, but simply by putting them together, you instantly narrow the field of possibilities. You now have, at the very least, a time period, and a focus. Something mysterious happened during WWII. Try to focus it a little more. Is it personal, or is it sweeping? WWII was certainly both. For the sake of example, say it's personal, one soldier's story.

When does it take place? WWII is obvious if it's about a WWII soldier's story—or is it? This is one of those decision points you will come to right away. Say it actually takes place now, which leads to the next question, "How now?". To move right along, lay out the beginning scenario: Your main character finds a journal—his grandfather's journal from WWII. This is a revelation, because Grandpa never made it home from the war, but nobody knows what happened. Perhaps, in this journal, your hero will uncover the answer.You now have several key questions answered, right out of the gate: who: your hero; when: then and now; what: a journal, and the mystery of a missing person. You don't know "why," yet. That is one of the things you must discover. How? Again, this must be uncovered through asking yourself questions.

Develop your characters: Start with the obvious. In this case, you have already created two characters—a young man and his grandfather. You can determine characteristics of both simply by the setting, and expand your characters in the process. Grandfather would likely have been married, so there would be a grandmother in the picture. There's a generation between grandpa and the young man, so there would be one of his parents who is also Grandpa's son or daughter. See how easy that is?

Continue along in this fashion, extending from one character to all the others that they may interact with. Before long, it's possible that you'll have too many characters and interactions. This is good, especially in a mystery. You may have need of "red shirts," like the hapless, disposable ensigns from the original Star Trek! In the process of developing your characters, you will likely ask yourself the same question your readers will soon be asking: what happens next? Use these questions to develop the story. You know, for your story, that the young man wants to find out what happened to Grandpa. Since all he has is the journal to go on, he reads it, and discovers Grandpa's story that lead him from his small town in Kentucky and his pregnant wife (grandma!), to the beaches of Normandy, to finding himself wounded behind enemy lines— all of which he wrote of in his journal. He never makes it home. Knowing these things, you see questions and a pattern emerge: Events take place in "today's" time, and also during WWII: As the journal is read, the date is 1944. As the grandson explores, it's today. To add some action to the mystery, the young man must do something. Since Grandpa isn't coming home, send the young man to Germany to find him— dead or alive.

Timeline your outline: Now that you've created the basic story (minus all the words), sketch your outline as a timeline, with each character's milestone events laid out on their own line. There will be times when two or more characters intersect, and where some disappear altogether. Just draw a line where those events happen. This too will give you something to kick start your muse when she falters.

Edit mercilessly: If you find your plot goes nowhere, and nothing you can do will help it— back up to where it last made sense, and try something else. Your story is not required to do anything you tell it to do in the outline. Sometimes, the story has other ideas where it wants to go. Wherever you are in the process, the muse may beckon you elsewhere. Follow her— this is part of the joy of writing.

WRITING A NOVEL

Write out the name of each chapter for your book and decide what you're going to put into it, that way you'll always know where you're going with the story.

Know the elements of a good novel: If you want to be a successful writer, think twice about taking creative writing as a course in college (unless you've already done so); instead, take English Literature. You have to know how to read with discernment and a critical eye before you write anything. Sentence structure, character distinction, plot formation, and character personality development all fall into place if you know how to read critically before you write.

Setting: The setting of a book is the time, place, and circumstances in which a story takes place. You don't need state this outright, of course. Like a painter might do, you create a picture in the mind of your reader by painting around the subject.

For example: Maria walked down the steep slope surrounding the castle. Before she could get very far, one of her father's maids stopped her and said, "King Ferdinand would like to see you." This suggests that Maria, possibly a young girl, lives on castle grounds. This would give the reader clues that the book might take place in medieval times. Maria is also a Latin name, which could suggest where she lives, and "King Ferdinand" is a giant clue! In fact, the wife of King Ferdinand—Isabel of Castile—approved and funded Christopher Columbus's voyage to the New World in about A.D. 1492, so this story probably takes place around that time.

Characters: Every story has major and minor characters. It's important that you make yours interesting and introduce them properly. Introducing the setting, and maybe even the characters, is called the exposition.

There are several types of characters that many books have. The protagonist is usually a main character and one that the book follows. For every protagonist, there is usually an antagonist, the character who provides the friction a story needs to proceed. The villains in books are generally antagonists, but not always.

Keep this in mind: very often, one man's villain is another man's hero. Regardless of the roles they play, these character types are important to make your story successful.

The conflict: A conflict is a large problem that a character faces, usually the reason for the story to exist in the first place. Maybe Maria, the King's daughter, has been asked to make the decision whether to let Columbus use Spanish ships and sailors for his adventures. She may continue to face this problem for most of the story.

The climax: The climax is the point of highest tension in the book, the point where the reader is really holding their breath.Perhaps Maria has just decided against letting Columbus use Spain's money to explore when he shows up, begging her to let him go and saying he'll do anything to have this chance. This is the point where Maria has a big choice to make, one that determines the whole outcome of the story.

The resolution: The climax is over, the problem has been solved, and any loose ends have been tied up. Note: if you intend to make a sequel, leave at least one or two loose ends unresolved. For the example here, Maria decides to honor Columbus's wishes, lets him go, and convinces her father to let her go with Columbus on his journey. It's often interesting for the reader if there is an ending you weren't expecting, so don't always make the ending of your book predictable. Details are some of the most important things to write in a book. Instead of just saying. "The sky was blue", say what kind of shade of blue it is, such as "The sky was a light shade of indigo." It can really boost the interest level of your story. But don't go overboard. A bad example would be: "The sky was a light shade of indigo, which set off the deep burnt onyx of the sands, flecked with effervescent spittle of foam from the lime-tinged aquamarine breakers." Over-the-top embellishment can make you look like you're trying too hard (and likely you are).

Be descriptive and light on your feet, and maybe add a poetic tone to your story.

Write out your plot: This will give you a starting point to anchor your story. Nothing fancy, just a general idea of what goes on. Halfway through the book, look over the original plot you wrote down. It'll be amazing how your perception of your book may have changed. You can change your book to match the original plot or scrap the plot and go with what you've written. You could even integrate and mix the two--whatever you want. Remember this is your book! Start writing! This is the best part. If you're having trouble starting, skip to the conflict of the story, and go from there. Once you feel comfortable with your writing, you can add the setting. You'll probably change loads of things in the story, because the great thing about writing a book is you can let your imagination run wild. The only thing you have to remember is that you have to enjoy the process, or your book will probably end up in a cylindrical metal container flecked with deep brick-colored oxidation and peeling shards of turquoise latex pigment (namely, a rusty old trash bin).

Remember that your notebook should only be used for planning! It is best to type up your story so you can create multiple copies of it, easily remove mistakes, and pitch it to publishers.

WRITING A NON-FICTION BOOK

Pick something you know, or want to know— about. Your nonfiction book could be information about a place where the reader might be vacationing, or information on a place in general. It could be about today's society, or a contemporary or historical leader or person of interest. The only caveat for true non-fiction is that it be factual.

Research: As much as they may know, every expert has at least one new thing to learn! You can never know too much about a subject. If you are having trouble or reach a stumbling block, try these things:

Go online: Sometimes it will take a bit of digging to narrow things down, but let the search engines of the world help you in your knowledge quest. Follow not just the main articles, but the referenced articles as well. Leave questions on forums and other places in case anyone can help you resolve them.

Read another non-fiction book about, or related to your subject. The author may see things from a different perspective, and may have some information you were not aware of, which you will duly confirm from an independent source before including it in your story, right? Right!

Ask an expert: There is likely an expert in the field who has made it their life's work to know everything about the topic you're writing on. Seek them out, honor their time, and ask them if there is something that might be unique and interesting about your subject.

Read an encyclopedia: Yes, it's a boring job, but somebody's got to do it. It might as well be you, as you gather all the information you need for your book.

Format your book: The books that don't get published are the ones that are poorly organized. For example, don't talk about good places to fish and good beaches in Europe in the same chapter.

Add copious descriptive details: No one wants to read a boring book! Good books are enriched with details and color.

KEEP AT IT

Be persistent: A cabbie was stopped by a young man in Manhattan who asked, "How do I get to Carnegie Hall?" "Practice," replied the cabbie. Practice makes perfect. Write constantly—whether it's your story, or just a thought or an observation. The more you do it, the better you'll get. It doesn't have to be perfect, it doesn't have to read how you want it to initially––what matters most is getting it out. There will be plenty of time to review the approaches to writing taken later. Keep asking questions of your motives, your story, and your characters. Everything and everyone in your novel should have a reason for being there— saying the leaves are green shows the readers it's spring or summer. Saying the character had a three-day beard shows that he's under duress of some sort (or he's a Hollywood actor). Every character has a motivation for what they do, so ask "them" as you write. "Why are you about to get on that plane and leave him alone in Morocco?"

Take breaks to get back some perspective: Writing improves with distance. On returning to it, you'll often see what works and doesn't work in your written piece, whereas trying to perceive this when you're stuck in the middle of it is a lot harder. Set aside a chapter for a week and come back to it later, refreshed and with new eyes. If you get writer's block, stop writing for a few days or so, and listen to some calming music to clear your head.

Find opinions other than your own: Let other people read your book's manuscript. They can give you valuable feedback, and perhaps even help you as you continue to write. Ditch what doesn't work. Unsurprisingly, there will be plenty that doesn't work. Don't be afraid to delete characters, plots and anything else from your book if it isn't working. Equally, don't be afraid to add new elements and characters that seem to bridge gaps and give sense to what you're writing. In the case of non-fiction, never be afraid to find more facts to back up your statements. Remember that many authors fail at many drafts before they find an actual idea that's good enough to stick with. Take Veronica Roth, author of the Divergent trilogy. She says in her blog that it took her at least 48 tries to find an idea to stick with, and that was in college!

Write what you know: This old saying can either work for you or not. It's good to not need to do a whole bunch of research before writing, but a little doesn't hurt. Also, it's a good exercise: Writing new things could help unearth an idea.

Keep at it: Try to make your mind churn out ideas all the time, so you never have an excuse not to write. You don't need to fit EVERYTHING into your story, just enough to satisfy the reader. If you get sick of writing, and just come to a stop, take a break and re-connect with the world outside, where you get some ideas from. Or try free-form writing-just write, no edits, no erasing "because it sounds bad" just write, write, write, - even if they are scattered scenes, rhymes, or two words

CHAPTER 6:
STRATEGIES FOR
ORGANIZATION

The description of strong writing varies in different parts of the world. Just as values for many other topics change from culture to culture, what constitutes good writing also changes. It is therefore important to help your students write well in English and to teach them what strong writing in English looks like. In English one of the most important strategies in writing is organization of content. A strong English writer is a guide to his or her reader leading him or her along the logical arguments in the piece. Following are six ways to do this effectively. If your students can understand and apply these organizational strategies, they will be far along the road to successful writing in English.

Chronology

Chronology, or time, is the most straightforward way to organize content in a piece of writing. Students should easily grasp the concept of starting at the earliest historical event and progressing toward the most recent or vice versa. This is also a good organization strategy when examining the change in one element (e.g. gender in literature) over time or to show how one idea, place or thing has changed over time. Items can be placed in either forward or reverse chronological order. In other words, events can be placed in order from first to last or from last to first. Typically, when organizing events chronologically, it is important to start with main sections of time and then further divides those sections into subsections. For example, when writing about history, include certain spans of years, such as decades, and then list events as they occurred within those decades. Because items or events are placed in order according to time, it helps individuals understand sequence and its effect on events. It gives an audience the opportunity to grasp cause-and-effect relationships and reasons for certain occurrences.

Familiarity and Importance

Unlike chronology, organizing content by either familiarity or importance is more subjective. In this type of organization, students begin with the most familiar topic or concept and move toward the most obscure, the least important toward the most important. They can also begin with the most simple and move to the most complex. This type of organization will build momentum in writing. You should warn your students to always keep in mind the target audience when organizing by familiarity to be most effective. Though eating frog may be quite familiar in a restaurant in Beijing, most Americans have not ever had the experience and would view the idea of it quite unfamiliar. It would therefore be placed toward the end of the written piece.

Compare and Contrast

Comparisons look at the similarities between two or more items, contrasts look at the differences. Though an organizational strategy may be to compare and contrast, stress to your students that this is never the purpose in writing. This organizational strategy works well when the writer is trying to present one item as superior to another, to explain an unknown item by comparing it to a known item, or to show how something has changed. Most academic papers both compare and contrast rather than focusing on just one or the other. There are two ways to organize writing when comparing and contrasting. A point by point organization takes each element of comparison or contrast and examines both items in relation to it separately. For example, a writer may examine the science of both food and beauty, then the social roles of food and beauty and then the psychological importance of both food and beauty. A block organization, on the other hand, presents all the information about one item before moving on to the next. In the same piece, block organization would present the topic of food and examine its science, social role and psychological importance. Then the writer would examine beauty on those same three points. If students are comparing more than two points, point by point organization will be more effective.

General and Particular

This type of organization takes broad generalizations and moves towards specific statements or starts with specific statements and compiles them into a general conclusion or statement. This is not the same as having a thesis statement and supporting it with details. One example of broad to general would be to examine the short stories of Edgar Allen Poe as a whole and move towards specific issues he includes in this writing such as death and revenge. Narrow to broad examination might begin examining state laws and then move to national laws. This type of organization can be used effectively when examining a larger item along with its component pieces.

Problem and Solution

A more straightforward organization examines the relationships between problems and solutions. This type of organization will do one of two things. It will state a problem and offer multiple solutions concluding with a recommendation or it will begin with a question, make multiple proposals or attempts and conclude with the outcome. This type of organization is most effective with scientific research where the writer formulates a hypothesis, evaluates the proposals and concludes with a solution to the problem.

Cause and Effect

A cause and effect organizational strategy examines the causal relationships throughout a paper. There are three ways to organize with a cause and effect scheme. The first begins with one event and examines the multiple causes. For example, a student may want to discuss the causes of drug abuse listing peer pressure, medical need and addictive tendencies in the argument. Another student may follow the second strategy which looks at the multiple effects of one course of action or cause. This student may look at the issue of high caloric intake and present the effects of weight gain, insulin imbalance and susceptibility to diabetes. A third strategy for cause and effect organization is a chain of causes and effects which begins with one event and follows the chain reaction to the end result. One example of this might be to examine the chain of events in which the assassination of Archduke Ferdinand led to World War I. Though the specific organizational strategy will have to be decided after the student determines the writing purpose, knowledge of these six organizational strategies will give your students the tools they need to communicate successfully in English. You may want to stick with chronology, familiarity and cause/effect with lower level students, but those who wish to be successful in academia or business would do well to understand all of them.

CHAPTER 7:
ALL THE RIGHT
INGREDIENTS

Centuries ago, Aristotle noted in his book Poetics that while a story does have a beginning, a middle and an ending, the beginning is not simply the first event in a series of three, but rather the emotionally engaging originating event. The middle is the natural and causally related consequence, and the end is the inevitable conclusive event. In other words, stories have an origination, an escalation of conflict, and a resolution. Of course, stories also need a vulnerable character, a setting that's integral to the narrative, meaningful choices that determine the outcome of the story, and reader empathy. But at its most basic level, a story is a transformation unveiled—either the transformation of a situation or, most commonly, the transformation of a character. Simply put, you do not have a story until something goes wrong. At its heart, a story is about a person dealing with tension, and tension is created by unfulfilled desire. Without forces of antagonism, without setbacks, without a crisis event that initiates the action, you have no story. The secret, then, to writing a story that draws readers in and keeps them turning pages is not to make more and more things happen to a character, and especially not to follow some preordained plot formula or novel-writing template. Instead, the key to writing better stories is to focus on creating more and more tension as your story unfolds.

Understanding the fundamentals at the heart of all good stories will help you tell your own stories better—and sell more of them, too. Imagine you're baking a cake. You mix together certain ingredients in a specific order and end up with a product that is uniquely different than any individual ingredient. In the process of mixing and then baking the cake, these ingredients are transformed into something delicious. That's what you're trying to do when you make up a story. So let's look at five essential story ingredients, and then review how to mix them together to make your story so good readers will ask for seconds.

Ingredient 1: Orientation

The beginning of a story must grab the reader's attention, orient her to the setting, mood and tone of the story, and introduce her to a protagonist she will care about, even worry about, and emotionally invest time and attention into. If readers don't care about your protagonist, they won't care about your story, either. So, what's the best way to introduce this all-important character? In essence, you want to set reader expectations and reveal a portrait of the main character by giving readers a glimpse of her normal life. If your protagonist is a detective, we want to see him at a crime scene. If you're writing romance, we want to see normal life for the young woman who's searching for love. Whatever portrait you draw of your character's life, keep in mind that it will also serve as a promise to your readers of the transformation that this character will undergo as the story progresses. For example, if you introduce us to your main character, Frank, the happily married man next door, readers instinctively know that Frank's idyllic life is about to be turned upside down—most likely by the death of either his spouse or his marriage. Something will soon rock the boat and he will be altered forever. Because when we read about harmony at the start of a story, it's a promise that discord is about to come. Readers expect this. Please note that normal life doesn't mean pain-free life. The story might begin while your protagonist is depressed, hopeless, grieving or trapped in a sinking submarine. Such circumstances could be what's typical for your character at this moment. When that happens, it's usually another crisis (whether internal or external) that will serve to kick-start the story. Which brings us to the second ingredient.

Ingredient 2: Crisis:

This crisis that tips your character's world upside down must, of course, be one that your protagonist cannot immediately solve. It's an unavoidable, irrevocable challenge that sets the movement of the story into motion. Typically, your protagonist will have the harmony of both his external world and his internal world upset by the crisis that initiates the story. One of these two imbalances might have happened before the beginning of the story, but usually at least one will occur on the page for your readers to experience with your protagonist, and the interplay of these two dynamics will drive the story forward. Depending on the genre, the crisis that alters your character's world might be a call to adventure—a quest that leads to a new land, or a prophecy or revelation that he's destined for great things. Mythic, fantasy and science-fiction novels often follow this pattern. In crime fiction, the crisis might be a new assignment to a seemingly unsolvable case. In romance, the crisis might be undergoing a divorce or breaking off an engagement. In each case, though, life is changed and it will never be the same again. George gets fired. Amber's son is kidnapped. Larry finds out his cancer is terminal. Whatever it is, the normal life of the character is forever altered, and she is forced to deal with the difficulties that this crisis brings. There are two primary ways to introduce a crisis into your story. Either begins the story by letting your character have what he desires most and then ripping it away, or by denying him what he desires most and then dangling it in front of him. So, he'll either lose something vital and spend the story trying to regain it, or he'll see something desirable and spend the story trying to obtain it.

Say you've imagined a character who desires love more than anything else. His deepest fear will be abandonment. You'll either want to introduce the character by showing him in a satisfying, loving relationship, and then insert a crisis that destroys it, or you'll want to show the character's initial longing for a mate, and then dangle a promising relationship just out of his reach so that he can pursue it throughout the story. Likewise, if your character desires freedom most, then he'll try to avoid enslavement. So, you might begin by showing that he's free, and then enslave him, or begin by showing that he's enslaved, and then thrust him into a freedom-pursuing adventure. It all has to do with what the main character desires, and what he wishes to avoid.

Ingredient 3: Escalation

There are two types of characters in every story—pebble people and putty people. If you take a pebble and throw it against a wall, it'll bounce off the wall unchanged. But if you throw a ball of putty against a wall hard enough, it will change shape. Always in a story, your main character needs to be a putty person. When you throw him into the crisis of the story, he is forever changed, and he will take whatever steps he can to try and solve his struggle—that is, to get back to his original shape (life before the crisis). But he will fail, Because he'll always be a different shape at the end of the story than he was at the beginning. If he's not, readers won't be satisfied. Putty people are altered, Pebble people remain the same. They're like set pieces. They appear onstage in the story, but they don't change in essential ways as the story progresses. They're the same at the ending as they were at the beginning. And they are not very interesting, exactly what kind of wall are we throwing our putty person against? First, stop thinking of plot in terms of what happens in your story. Rather, think of it as payoff for the promises you've made early in the story. Plot is the journey toward transformation. As I mentioned earlier, typically two crisis events interweave to form the multilayered stories that today's readers expect: an external struggle that needs to be overcome, and an internal struggle that needs to be resolved. As your story progresses, then, the consequences of not solving those two struggles need to become more and more intimate, personal and devastating. If you do this, then as the stakes are raised, the two struggles will serve to drive the story forward and deepen reader engagement and interest. Usually if a reader says she's bored or that "nothing's happening in the story," she doesn't necessarily mean that events aren't occurring, but rather that she doesn't see the protagonist taking natural, logical steps to try and solve his struggle. During the escalation stage of your story, let your character take steps to try and resolve the two crises (internal and external) and get back to the way things were earlier, before his world Was tipped upside down.

Ingredient 4: Discovery

At the climax of the story, the protagonist will make a discovery that changes his life. Typically, this discovery will be made through wit (as the character cleverly pieces together clues from earlier in the story) or grit (as the character shows extraordinary perseverance or tenacity) to overcome the crisis event (or meet the calling) he's been given. The internal discovery and the external resolution help reshape our putty person's life and circumstances forever. The protagonist's discovery must come from a choice that she makes, not simply by chance or from a Wise Answer-Giver. While mentors might guide a character toward self-discovery, the decisions and courage that determine the outcome of the story must come from the protagonist. In one of the paradoxes of storytelling, the reader wants to predict how the story will end (or how it will get to the end), but he wants to be wrong. So, the resolution of the story will be most satisfying when it ends in a way that is both inevitable and unexpected

Ingredient 5: Change

Think of a caterpillar entering a cocoon. Once he does so, one of two things will happen: He will either transform into a butterfly, or he will die. But no matter what else happens, he will never climb out of the cocoon as a caterpillar. So it is with your protagonist. As you frame your story and develop your character, ask yourself, "What is my caterpillar doing?" Your character will either be transformed into someone more mature, insightful or at peace, or will plunge into death or despair. Although genre can dictate the direction of this transformation—horror stories will often end with some kind of death (physical, psychological, emotional or spiritual)—most genres are butterfly genres. Most stories end with the protagonist experiencing new life— whether that's physical renewal, psychological understanding, emotional healing or a spiritual awakening. This change marks the resolution of the crisis and the culmination of the story.

As a result of facing the struggle and making this new discovery, the character will move to a new normal. The character's actions or attitude at the story's end show us how she's changed from the story's inception. The putty has become a new shape, and if it's thrown against the wall again, the reader will understand that a brand-new story is now unfolding. The old way of life has been forever changed by the process of moving through the struggle to the discovery and into a new and different life.

LETTING STRUCTURE FOLLOW STORY

I don't have any idea how many acts my novels contain. A great many writing instructors, classes and manuals teach that all stories should have three acts—and, honestly, that doesn't make much sense to me. After all, in theater, you'll find successful one-act, two-act, three-act and four-act plays. And most assuredly, they are all stories. If you're writing a novel that people won't read in one sitting (which is presumably every novel), your readers couldn't care less about how many acts there are—in fact, they probably won't even be able to keep track of them. What readers really care about is the forward movement of the story as it escalates to its inevitable and unexpected conclusion. While it's true that structuring techniques can be helpful tools, unfortunately, formulaic approaches frequently send stories spiraling off in the wrong direction or, just as bad, handcuff the narrative flow. Often the people who advocate funneling your story into a predetermined three-act structure will note that stories have the potential to sag or stall out during the long second act. And whenever I hear that, I think, then why not shorten it? Or chop it up and include more acts? Why let the story suffer just so you can follow a formula? I have a feeling that if you asked the people who teach three-act structure if they'd rather have a story that closely follows their format, or one that intimately connects with readers, they would go with the latter. Why? Because I'm guessing that deep down, even they know that in the end, story trumps structure.

Once I was speaking with another writing instructor and he told me that the three acts form the skeleton of a story. I wasn't sure how to respond to that until I was at an aquarium with my daughter later that week and I saw an octopus. I realized that it got along pretty well without a skeleton. A storyteller's goal is to give life to a story, not to stick in bones that aren't necessary for that species of tale. So, stop thinking of a story as something that happens in three acts, or two acts, or four or seven, or as something that is driven by predetermined elements of plot. Rather, think of your story as an organic whole that reveals a transformation in the life of your character. The number of acts or events should be determined by the movement of the story, not the other way around.

Because story trumps structure:

If you render a portrait of the protagonist's life in such a way that we can picture his world and also care about what happens to him, we'll be drawn into the story. If you present us with an emotionally stirring crisis or calling, we'll get hooked. If you show the stakes rising as the character struggles to solve this crisis, you'll draw us in more deeply. And if you end the story in a surprising yet logical way that reveals a transformation of the main character's life, we'll be satisfied and anxious to read your next story.

The ingredients come together, and the cake tastes good.

Always be ready to avoid formulas, discard acts and break the "rules" for the sake of the story—which is another way of saying: Always be ready to do it for the sake of your readers.

CHAPTER 8:
THE WRITING PROCESS: YOU CAN DO IT

The advice of creative writing includes the birth of a novel, the process, writing a scene, experience palettes to paint from, running themes, make your reader invest, the self-writing novel and weaving the twists and turns. It's time to take a peek at that scary diagram again. Writing fiction is really not much different from travel writing. In travel writing you go off to a place and spend X number of months/years there and take notes on what you see and who you meet and then distil all this into a book. In fiction writing you do exactly the same. The only difference is that the places and people don't exist. You create an entire world in your head and spend X number of months there and then you write about it. That's not to say you won't travel to real places and meet real people in order to help make your fictional world real. At the end of the writing process, when you have a completed manuscript, it should feel like you were actually there. It should be the case that you can turn to people who read about your world and say to them, "there's so much more I could tell you.' We've already looked at how there's no single starting point to a novel. However, after the idea takes root and starts to grow, there are three sections that will begin to take shape. Usually you will end up with an initial notes document that has the early stages of these upon it:

Characters: A few basic thoughts about the main characters, names, relationship to each other, age, gender, nationality etc.

Key scenes/dialogue: Often a particular key scene, event or significant piece of dialogue will come into being at the very earliest stages.

Timeline/plot: A basic overview of what might happen in the novel should also start to take shape. This is our start. By taking it slowly and walking logically through the process, you will calmly and comfortably amass a lot of material and suddenly find a novel falls out the end of it.

RESEARCH

As soon as anything pops into your head, research it. You want to write a scene set in a market? Walk round a dozen markets. Find out about the rules and regulations, observe, sketch, photograph. Take in the noise and smells that hit you. Become an expert in markets. You'll notice from the diagram that the research pile of papers looks bigger than the novel itself. That's how it should be. Your manuscript is the water balloon, the research is the water. If your manuscript expands too much without enough research then it's just hot air. A water bomb with only a little water in it that is mainly just hot air doesn't make much of a splash. Everything in your novel should come from four sources:

Knowledge: Something you just happen to know -- it might come from a film or documentary you once saw or just from talking with friends. But, how well do you know it? If it's hazy then research it.

Experience: Something that happened to you that you can draw on. But you could still research and find out other people's experiences of the same thing if it's a major plot element.

Research: Something you know little or nothing about and so you look it up or consult an expert.

Original concept: Something that no one has written about or ever dreamed up so it's up to you to chart unknown territory. However, you need to thoroughly check this out and research anything similar to help guide you. Only something completely original should come off the top of your head -- everything else should be researched thoroughly.

Characters: Once you start to grow this list beyond the most basic "stars' of the book then it's best to strip this list out as a separate document. For each character write as much info as possible. You should also have a lot of back history written that won't necessarily go into the novel but ensures you know them inside out. Write a small biography of them, write about their personality and characteristics, their likes and dislikes. Are there any key phrases that they say a lot?

Locations: This is where your scenes will happen. Whatever type of location you choose for each scene, research it thoroughly. Visit as many examples of these types of locations as you can. Even if it's an environment that you are familiar with, revisit it time and time again and switch on all your senses, absorb even the most trivial of details. Keep a list of your fictional locations with details of what happens there. Each location might have it's own timeline of events that happen there. From your locations list, start to draw up maps and diagrams. Don't just set a scene in a generic "office.' Is it an old office? A new office? Tidy? Cluttered? Noisy?

Quiet? What's on the walls? Draw a diagram of the seating layout and the doors windows etc. This will stop you writing illogical scenes further down the line. It will also cause you to think about your characters interacting in this environment and help prevent your scenes growing stale.

Novel/Chronological timeline: This is the sequence of events in order. Even if your plot is going to flow through in natural chronological order there should still be 2 timelines. Your chronological timeline will include all the events from your book in time order plus some additional events that occur during your plot that you may not write about but need to be considered. The Novel timeline will be a list of events in the order the novel will present them to the reader, so it might well jump about in time. At some point, when this list is complete, you can start separating out and/or grouping these events until a very rough guide to the chapters begins to take shape.

Now we can attempt to put together the basic skeleton of the manuscript. Take your Novel timeline and save it as a separate document (You need to keep the original basic list to refer back to as an overview). Call this new document draft_01. Hit a load of returns between all the points to separate out your chapters. Now take any key scenes and bits of dialogue and paste them in where they need to go (they can always be moved later). Any new scenes or dialogue you think up you can write directly into the manuscript. With Nix Ex Machina, the novel became so big that the spelling/grammar underlines failed due to memory issues. For this reason I split the chapters into separate word documents, but early on it's good to have the whole thing in one place so you can leap around the plot. It's tempting now to think that you're away -- that you can just keep the research up, keep adding characters and expand the text in your manuscript according to the timeline points until you have a finished first draft. You could do that. But in order to add a bit more depth to it, there are four more documents we need to start building up as we write the novel:

Character psychoses: How do the events affect our characters. Who they start off as at the beginning will probably have changed by the end. For each character, map a timeline of their emotions and motivations, how these change and what effect other characters have on them and how they in turn affect others.

Location themes: So you've invented a dusty warehouse where some gangsters hang out...

create a list of metaphors that help lift the location above the mundane and give it that edge of realism. These metaphorical themes will help you write consistently about the places. Example: An old office where there are a lot of empty desks. It is a ghost ship, not much moves but shadows seem to twitch through doorways, people talk here in whispers and the light here is dim, even on a sunny day. The predominant colours are black and grey with the odd hint of metal blue or faded brown. This place feels like a museum that you have broken into out of hours. You never feel comfortable here. The air is heavy and you breathe dust. Your footsteps echo down the corridors. There is always noise here, but it always seems to be in another room or on another floor, muffled in the distance like you are hearing voices from the past. See? With that metaphorical description of the office, each time you come to write a scene there a powerful image is in your head that will steer the atmosphere, rather than just writing another scene in "the empty old office.'

Baggage: This refers to those small issues that arise as you write the novel that you never bargained for but need to be dealt with. If some emotional event happens in one chapter than there will be a natural follow-through process needed to make sure this event causes the ripples it would in later parts of the book. Put very simply, there's no point writing about someone's partner dying and then starting the next chapter "John woke up feeling happy with a good feeling inside." Keep a track of what baggage each character is carrying. We'll cover this in greater depth in the section 'The self-writing novel.'

Running themes: This is similar to the character psychoses and the location themes but covers recurring plot themes that are not character or place dependent. These are metaphorical themes that run throughout your novel and add another artistic layer to your text.

They fall into two categories:

Natural themes: These are themes that you notice have occurred in your novel naturally as you have written it.

Engineered themes: These are themes that you consciously decide to insert into your novel.

FIRST DRAFT

Once you follow this process through, you will end up with your first draft. Let's face it, it's the most terrifying thing a writer faces. Which often leads to the most terrifying thing writer's face: a first draft so utterly, irredeemably discombobulated that in retrospect that empty white screen seems soothing, inviting almost. And yet, as Hemingway said with such blunt eloquence, "All first drafts are shit." Very true. All first drafts have plot holes, places where character motivation goes missing, dull scenes, clunky transgressions and unearned epiphanies.

But there's a huge difference between writing a draft of an actual story and simply "letting it all pour out and romping all over the place," as Anne Lamott advises writers to do in Bird by Bird. I know, Lamott's book is fabulous and she makes a gazillion great points, but this one has been universally misinterpreted, undermining thousands of writers, many of whom may have given up as a result and actually gone to dental school. Not that there's anything wrong with dental school, mind you. But sheesh, the thought of a potential F. Scott Fitzgerald scaling teeth is kind of sad.

So let's talk about the "let it pour out" definition of a "shitty first draft" — why it's so dangerous and so tempting, and what you can do to steer clear of it. Why are we tempted to "let it all pour out?" Because we're hardwired to do what's easy. It's not a negative, nor does it make us weak. It's a survival mechanism, the better to conserve energy for handling the decidedly unexpected. For that reason, as neuroscientist Antonio Damasio says, "smart brains are also extremely lazy. Anytime they can do less instead of more, they will, a minimalist philosophy they follow religiously. "Let's face it, it's much easier – seemingly liberating – to let 'er rip and write without thinking, pantser-style, than it is to think about what you're writing beforehand, and track it as you go. Plus, since staring at that blank page can be exceedingly stressful, the relief of letting it all pour out not only feels good, it feels right. Thus it's easy to believe that this is the natural path to storytelling. Which in turn means that if at the end of the day that flood can't be shaped into an actual story? Well, you must not be a real writer after all. Don't you believe it for a minute. Letting loose, regardless how good it feels, doesn't produce the kind of first draft that Hemingway was referring to. That is, a draft that begins to capture – in rudimentary, unpolished form – the story itself.

So rather than flying blind, here are nine tips that can help you create that sort of shitty first draft, as opposed to a bunch of pages with words randomly romping across them.

1. Don't worry about the language or "writing well," even for a moment. Don't

strain after metaphors, don't worry about symbolism, forget your love of language. Concentrate on what the language is meant to convey: the story itself. One of the biggest mistakes writers make is to begin polishing their first draft even before it's even finished. The more you polish at this stage, the deeper you'll fall in love with your words, and the harder it will be to kill your darlings. I recently spoke with a writer who was celebrating having finished the first draft of his novel. He told me proudly that it came in at a little over 100,000 words, and that he loved every single one of them. Uh oh.

2. Know what your point is before you begin to write. All stories make a point, and everything in a story – in one way or another – builds toward it. If you know what you're trying to say, chances are much better your story will actually communicate it. Plus, it will give you a yardstick by which you can gauge what's relevant, and what might be a darling you'll only have to steel yourself to whack later. Might your point change as you write? Absolutely. It's a first draft, nothing is written in stone. But even knowing what your point might be allows you to

focus in on a story that makes it, rather than romping aimlessly. A story making point moves, a story that romps tends to run in place.

3. Don't expect "the force" to write through you. You are not a channel for some otherworldly energy, you're a writer, and everything you write comes from you. You have the power to harness your prose to a story, and you have the power to then shape it, polish it, and change your reader's worldview by allowing them to experience the hard won change your protagonist goes through. Take responsibility. Is it harder to write this way? You bet. As Dorothy Parker noted, "I hate writing, I love having written." Sometimes that's the way it goes.

4. Know the overarching problem your protagonist will face. A story is about how someone solves a problem they can't avoid, and what he or she has to overcome, internally, in order to do it. It's this overarching problem that gives a story context. From the first page of Gone Girl we're wondering, "What's up with Amy and did Nick have anything to do with her disappearance?" The problem is

there front and center, and it's what hooks readers from the get-go. What's yours?

5. Know your ending first. If you don't know where your story is going, how will you have the slightest idea whether it's moving at all? How will you know what turns to take? How will you know what needs to happen next? Or at all? You won't. Without a target to aim for, chances are high your story will idle in neutral.

6. Know how your protagonist sees the world. If the overarching problem is what gives your story context, what gives it meaning is how your protagonist navigates that problem. In other words, how does your protagonist react to what happens? One of the most stubborn brain myths is that our brain is like a camera, recording an exact, objective account of everything we see. Not so. Rather, we record events in bits and pieces, subjectively, depending on what matters most to us. We then evaluate what we've "seen" based on what life has taught us thus far. If you don't know what has shaped your protagonist's worldview, how will you know how she'll react to anything that happens? Or why? Your reader will

be getting to know your protagonist on the first page, but you need to know her inside and out long before you commit her to paper.

7. Find your story's third rail, and make sure everything touches it. Here is the essence of a story: the protagonist is forced, by circumstances outside her control, to deal with a problem she'd really rather avoid. This forces her to dig deep and overcome the inner issue, wound or misconception that's holding her back. Everything in the story impacts this quest. Think of it as your story's third rail – everything must touch it, giving it juice and causing sparks to fly. That means if what happens doesn't affect it in some way, no matter how well written it is, the story stalls. Find the live rail, it won't let you down. Once you zero in on it, it becomes a live sensor that beeps madly when the connection is broken.

8. Concentrate on the "why" and not the "what." This is a simple, incredibly useful one, even if you ignore the others. Whenever something is about to happen, ask yourself, "why?" Why is this happening now? Why is my protagonist

reacting the way she does? Why does the reader need to know this? Stories aren't about "what" happens, they're about "why." Just like life. Watch as your day unfolds. People do things – that's the what – but aren't you always wondering why they did it, what they really mean by it, so you can figure out what the heck you should do in response? In a story the most important initial "why" is why the protagonist wants what she wants, and why she can't seem to get it. Figure it out first, and it will be your true north.

9. Know your basic theme. This is much easier than it sounds. Think of theme as what your story is saying about human nature, which is reflected in how people treat each other in the world you're creating. Characters' actions – and therefore what's humanly possible – are going to be very different in the world of a lighthearted romance from that of a dystopian drama. What world will your story unfold in? And are you sure all your characters got the memo?

The beauty of approaching your first draft as a story, rather than as romping words, is that it allows you to really, truly quiet the voice that says you'll never be a good writer. Because it's not about the writing. It's about zeroing in the story that you want to tell. What's more, when you've nailed down the specifics we've been discussing, very often the story does pour out. Because you know where it's going, you can feel the intoxicating rush of your own creative momentum. It's thrilling. Even so, you'll end up producing a shitty first draft. But the beauty of this kind of shitty first draft is that when it's finished, you won't have to sift through endless words, hoping to discover the fragments of a story – it will be there. In fact, this is the one and only thing that can cut down on time spent rewriting. If you think you hear an underlying drum beat here, a cautionary tale about the pitfalls of being a pantser, you're absolutely right. Yes, some writers can sit down and nail a story blindfolded. They have that innate skill, and tend to be successful out of the starting gate. Most of us – and that include most successful writers – don't have that innate sense of story. But we can develop it by mastering story and committing it to muscle memory — that muscle being the brain. Of course, that still doesn't make it easy.

CHAPTER 9:
FINISHING YOUR BOOK FAST

Novelists are the distance runners, the long-haul truckers, the transoceanic captains of the literary world. There is no sprinting through a novel, at least not for the novelist; there are simply too many characters, too many scenes, too many story lines and pages and sentences to be written—and then rewritten, revised and polished. Endurance is key to completing the task. Yet endurance is not enough, not nearly. Because reading the novel is also a marathon experience, and that means the primary goal of your revision process should be to take pains to create a human pace for the reader, a pace that alternately rushes, strides, saunters and lingers, according to the story's—and the reader's—needs. It's no small task to keep those narrative wheels rolling, but that's what you have to do, all the way from the title page to The End. As a novelist, you need concrete strategies to sustain you on that long haul—and to transform your first draft into a work that can stand up to the task. Here are four rules you can use to make sure your readers won't fall asleep, burn out or just give up before they finish the final chapter of your masterpiece.

Write the whole first draft first—and fast.

This first rule deals not so much with revision, but with resisting the impulse to revise as you write. This is difficult in large part because it means forgiving yourself for writing terrible prose. There's no way around it. Fast means sloppy—sloppy diction, syntax, grammar. Any damage suffered by your writer's ego, however, will come at a small cost compared to the benefits gained. Truth is, a quickly written draft produces a narrative with a clean trajectory. Think of it as a carpenter's chalk line, the graph of your story's arc. Your characters might remain undercooked and your subplots unexplored in this first go-through, but in working fast you have little choice but to hew close to the basic story line. As a result, you're saved from the tempting side-trails and seductive tangents that can derail your progress. (You can come back to those later, when your task is to spice up and thicken your characters and plot, to pursue all of their wonderful complications. Here's the point, once you've blasted through to the end of a book, you have a much better sense of what belongs in the beginning and middle sections. And to your great advantage you won't have wasted your time writing, revising and polishing unnecessary scenes that will only end up on the cutting-room floor. How fast is fast, you ask? Depends on the writer. My natural habit is to work slowly, but I wrote the first draft of my current manuscript in six months, an hour a day, five or six days a week. My objective was to write two pages each time I sat down, not so daunting a task once I absolved myself in advance for committing every writer's sin there is, many times, in every session. If you do the same—if you dedicate yourself to writing without self-editing—you'll be amazed at how soon that draft is finished. Then it's time for the rewrite, starting with the element that will sustain your readers on their own marathon: the action.

Evaluate the dramatic function of every scene or unit of action.

Readers can tell if a passage fails to advance the story in some way. If that's the case, they begin to skim, or worse, they toss the book aside. Therefore, the best way to start revising is to begin rereading your first draft and ask yourself this essential question at the opening of every chapter or scene: "What exactly happens here, and how does it surprise my character or offer some new perception to the reader?" Be sure every dramatized incident, whatever it is—a fight, a conversation or merely a silent moment in which a character ponders some issue—moves the story to a new place. When you find scenes that don't, you've found the first targets of your revision. In Kent Haruf's Plainsong, a small-town Colorado teacher goes out to visit a pair of old bachelor farmers/brothers and stuns them (and the readers, too) by asking if they'd be willing to take in a high school girl who's been kicked out of her home because she's pregnant. The two old men, understandably, are struck dumb. It's a lively scene; the teacher's request a surprise that sets into motion a key element of the novel's plot.

The next passage, however, is quiet. The teacher has left the farmhouse kitchen, and the two men put on their coats and go outside into the winter night to fix a broken water heater. An entire page is spent describing how they chop free the heater from ice that's formed in the water tank and how they relight the pilot—nearly 300 words during which the men don't say one thing to each other! Nor does the narrator offer insight into their thoughts. Can such a passage justify itself? Listen to how it ends and to how Haruf transitions into the inevitable conversation: So for a while they stood below the windmill in the failing light. The thirsty horses approached and peered at them and sniffed at the water and began to drink, sucking up long draughts of it. Afterward they stood back watching the two brothers, their eyes as large and luminous as perfect round knobs of mahogany glass.It was almost dark now. Only a thin violet band of light showed in the west on the low horizon. The passage in question may not advance the plot directly, but it does demonstrate the particular way these brothers communicate with each other: silently, through side-by-side labor. Also, its evocative language makes us feel as if the horses themselves are grateful, a feeling the reader—consciously or not—brings to the discussion the brothers are about to have concerning the girl. Scenes don't have to be highly dramatic in order to perform valuable work. Yet it's important that you examine them one by one, satisfying yourself that each will deepen your readers' connection to the story and urge them to turn the page.

Identify lulls in action where you can insert mini-scenes.

As novels progress, they inevitably alternate between the modes of scene and summary. Scenes, of course, depict moments of decision and high emotion, turning points that demand a full dramatic rendering, complete with dialogue, action and vivid descriptions. But intervening periods of time, lulls between episodes of heavy weather, character histories and complicated relationships also must be accounted for.

Summaries, then—long passages of exposition—are a necessary evil. (All that densely packed prose, with no white space for the eye to rest upon! One way to help your readers persevere through spots where the pacing lags is to spice up the passages with bits of live action, with mini-scenes. In the first chapter of Jon Hassler's Staggerford, the narrator spends pages describing a typical day in the life of Miles Pruitt, a high school English instructor—a tedious approach had Hassler not interjected several mini-scenes into the long summary. Notice how smoothly Hassler moves from exposition to a moment of dry humor. All it requires is a single transitional sentence with the marker had indicating the shift backward in time: William Mulholland was in this class. In the Staggerford Public Library every book having to do with physics, chemistry, statistics, or any other sort of cold-blooded calculation contained on its check-out card the name William Mulholland. ... Only once had he spoken in this class. On the opening day of school Miles, taking roll, had said, "Bill Mulholland.""My name is William," he replied.

Toni Morrison uses a similar strategy throughout Beloved, a novel with a complex structure and wide scope that requires frequent use of summary. In this passage Sethe, a former slave, is reminiscing about her lost husband, Halle, and about other slaves she knew on the plantation. Morrison doesn't use transitional language at all. She simply plugs in a bit of uttered speech: Hidden behind honeysuckle she watched them. How different they were without her, how they laughed and played and urinated and sang. All but Sixo, who laughed once—at the very end. Halle, of course, was the nicest. Baby Suggs' eighth and last child, who rented himself out all over the country to buy her away from there. But he too, as it turned out, was nothing but a man."A man ain't nothing but a man," said Baby Suggs. "But a son? Well now, that's somebody." Be on the alert, then, in your own work for long paragraphs consisting of backstory, physical description and character analysis. The information in such passages may be necessary, but unless you sprinkle in memorable scenic elements—snippets of dialogue, little clips of movement— your readers might lose patience.

Vary your methods of beginning chapters.

Chapter breaks and other pauses allow readers to catch their breath, ponder what they've read and anticipate what might be coming next. As you revise your novel, don't miss the opportunity to look at them collectively and make sure you're offering a variety of chapter kickoffs to pique your readers. Sometimes you'll want to give them what they expect—but a good novelist walks the line between keeping readers comfortable and making them crazy, so other times it's best to startle them.

The most common method of getting a chapter started, one that takes readers by the hand and gently guides them into the next section of the story, is to position a character in time and instantly establish the dramatic situation. There's nothing flashy about this strategy, but it gets the job done.

On the morning of the 22nd I wakened with a start. Before I opened my eyes, I seemed to know that something had happened. I heard excited voices in the kitchen—grandmother's was so shrill that I knew she must be almost beside herself.

—Willa Cather, from Chapter 14 of My ÁntoniaAfter Ty left, it took me half an hour to get myself down to my father's.

—Jane Smiley, from Chapter 16 of A Thousand Acres

Another method sketches out a period of time, rendering its mood and general character as a way to place coming events into context. Use this strategy when your novel calls for a moment of reflection, requires a bit of backstory or needs to make a chronological leap forward. Here's F. Scott Fitzgerald at his evocative best: There was music from my neighbor's house through the summer nights. In his blue gardens men and girls came and went like moths among the whisperings and the champagne and the stars. Other times, though—especially following chapters that move at a leisurely pace—you'll feel the need to shake things up, toss readers in over their heads, pitch them a curve. In other words, crank up the speed a notch or two. In my novel Undiscovered Country, Chapter 13 begins with the appearance of the narrator's dead father in a moment for which neither the narrator nor the reader is prepared. This time he didn't smell like gunpowder and beeswax, but instead like he'd smelled on those nights when he got home late from closing and came into my room to check on me. ... He always reeked of cigarettes from his night at the Valhalla, but there was also a hint of his spearmint toothpaste and the soap he was partial to, a tangy brown bar soap peppered with mysterious black granules. It was this combination of smells that made me glance up now into the rearview mirror as Charlie and I neared the edge of town.Dad was in the backseat watching me.

Finally, a clever way to open a chapter is to offer some pithy observation that bears directly upon the events unfolding. Happy families are all alike; every unhappy family is unhappy in its own way. Remember that every new chapter offers the opportunity to reintroduce your story and re-orient your readers to the world of your novel. So as you revise, be strategic with your chapter openings. Your efforts will stave off reader complacency and give your novel the chance to hook your readers again and again. Are these all strategies you could employ while you write the first draft? I don't think so. It's not until you can stand back and look at that draft as a cohesive whole that you will be able to apply these rules effectively and give your manuscript the revision it requires. Writing and revising a novel means hard work, months or years of it— all the more reason to keep your readers' needs at the forefront of your mind as you're working. The time and energy invested in your novel doesn't come to an end, after all, once you revise the last page, or even after the manuscript has been edited, produced and published—because, finally, your readers pour themselves into it, lay their own claims to it. Keeping this in mind should inspire us to fashion novels that are enjoyable yet challenging, familiar yet surprising, and as free of unnecessary hindrances as we can make them.

CHAPTER 10:
GETTING YOUR BOOK PUBLISHED

Publishing is the process of production and dissemination of literature, music, or information — the activity of making information available to the general public. In some cases, authors may be their own publishers, meaning: originators and developers of content also provide media to deliver and display the content for the same. Also, the word publisher can refer to the individual who leads a publishing company or an imprint or to a person who owns/heads a magazine. Traditionally, the term refers to the distribution of printed works such as books (the "book trade") and newspapers. With the advent of digital information systems and the Internet, the scope of publishing has expanded to include electronic resources, such as the electronic versions of books and periodicals, as well as micropublishing, websites, blogs, video game publishers and the like. Publishing includes the stages of the development, acquisition, copy editing, graphic design, production – printing (and its electronic equivalents), and marketing and distribution of newspapers, magazines, books, literary works, musical works, software and other works dealing with information, including the electronic media.

Publication is also important as a legal concept:

- As the process of giving formal notice to the world of a significant intention, for example, to marry or enter bankruptcy;

- As the essential precondition of being able to claim defamation; that is, the alleged libel must have been published, and

- for copyright purposes, where there is a difference in the protection of published and unpublished works.

There are two categories of publisher:

1. Non-Paid Publishers: The term non-paid publisher refers to those publication houses which do not charge author at all to publish the book.

2. Paid Publishers: The author has to meet with the total expense to get the book published and author has full right to set up marketing policies. This is also known as vanity publishing.

THE PROCESS OF PUBLISHING

Book and magazine publishers spend a lot of their time buying or commissioning copy; newspaper publishers, by contrast, usually hire their own staff to produce copy, although they may also employ freelance journalists, called stringers. At a small press, it is possible to survive by relying entirely on commissioned material. But as activity increases, the need for works may outstrip the publisher's established circle of writers. For works written independently of the publisher, writers often first submit a query letter or proposal directly to a literary agent or to a publisher. Submissions sent directly to a publisher are referred to as unsolicited submissions, and the majority come from previously unpublished authors. If the publisher accepts unsolicited manuscripts, then the manuscript is placed in the slush pile, which publisher's readers sift through to identify manuscripts of sufficient quality or revenue potential to be referred to acquisitions editors for review. The acquisitions editors send their choices to the editorial staff. The time and number of people involved in the process is dependent on the size of the publishing company, with larger companies having more degrees of assessment between unsolicited submission and publication. Unsolicited submissions have a very low rate of acceptance, with some sources estimating that publishers ultimately choose about three out of every ten thousand unsolicited manuscripts they receive.

Many book publishing companies around the world maintain a strict "no unsolicited submissions" policy and will only accept submissions via a literary agent. This shifts the burden of assessing and developing writers out of the publishing company and onto the literary agents. At these companies, unsolicited manuscripts are thrown out, or sometimes returned, if the author has provided pre-paid postage. Established authors are often represented by a literary agent to market their work to publishers and negotiate contracts. Literary agents take a percentage of author earnings (varying between 10 to 15 percent) to pay for their services. Some writers follow a non-standard route to publication. For example, this may include bloggers who have attracted large readerships producing a book based on their websites, books based on Internet memes, instant "celebrities" such as Joe the Plumber, retiring sports figures and in general anyone a publisher feels could produce a marketable book. Such books often employ the services of a ghostwriter. For a submission to reach publication it must be championed by an editor or publisher who must work to convince other staff of the need to publish a particular title. An editor who discovers or champions a book that subsequently becomes a best-seller may find their own reputation enhanced as a result of their success.

Acceptance and negotiation

Once a work is accepted, commissioning editors negotiate the purchase of intellectual property rights and agree on royalty rates. The authors of traditional printed materials typically sell exclusive territorial intellectual property rights that match the list of countries in which distribution is proposed (i.e. the rights match the legal systems under which copyright protections can be enforced). In the case of books, the publisher and writer must also agree on the intended formats of publication —mass-market paperback, "trade" paperback and hardback is the most common options. The situation is slightly more complex, if electronic formatting is to be used. Where distribution is to be by CD-ROM or other physical media, there is no reason to treat this form differently from a paper format, and a national copyright is an acceptable approach. But the possibility of Internet download without the ability to restrict physical distribution within national boundaries presents legal problems that are usually solved by selling language or translation rights rather than national rights. Thus, Internet access across the European Union is relatively open because of the laws forbidding discrimination based on nationality, but the fact of publication in, say, France, limits the target market to those who read French. Having agreed on the scope of the publication and the formats, the parties in a book agreement must then agree on royalty rates, the percentage of the gross retail price that will be paid to the author, and the advance payment. This is difficult because the publisher must estimate the potential sales in each market and balance projected revenue against production costs. Royalties usually range between 10–12% of recommended retail price. An advance is usually 1/3 of first print run total royalties. For example, if a book has a print run of 5000 copies and will be sold at $14.95 and the author is to receive 10% royalties, the total sum payable to the author if all copies are sold is $7475 (10% x $14.95 x 5000). The advance in this instance would roughly be $2490. Advances vary greatly between books, with established authors commanding large advances.

Pre-production stages

Although listed as distinct stages, parts of these occur concurrently. As editing of text progresses, front cover design and initial layout takes place and sales and marketing of the book begins.

Editorial stage

A decision is taken to publish a work, and the technical legal issues resolved, the author may be asked to improve the quality of the work through rewriting or smaller changes, and the staff will edit the work. Publishers may maintain a house style, and staff will copy edit to ensure that the work matches the style and grammatical requirements of each market. Editors often choose or refine titles and headlines. Editing may also involve structural changes and requests for more information. Some publishers employ fact checkers, particularly regarding non-fiction works.

Design stage

When a final text is agreed upon, the next phase is design. This may include artwork being commissioned or confirmation of layout. In publishing, the word "art" also indicates photographs. Depending on the number of photographs required by the work, photographs may also be licensed from photo libraries. For those works that are particularly rich in illustrations the publisher may contract a picture researcher to find and license the photographs required for the work. The design process prepares the work for printing through processes such as typesetting, dust jacket composition, specification of paper quality, binding method and casing. The type of book being produced determines the amount of design required. For standard fiction titles, design is usually restricted to typography and cover design. For books containing illustrations or images, design takes on a much larger role in laying out how the page looks, how chapters begin and end, colors, typography, cover design and ancillary materials such as posters, catalogue images and other sales materials. Non-fiction illustrated titles are the most design intensive books, requiring extensive use of images and illustrations, captions, typography and a deep involvement and consideration of the reader experience. The activities of typesetting, page layout, the production of negatives, plates from the negatives and, for hardbacks, the preparation of brasses for the spine legend and Imprint are now all computerized. Prepress computerization evolved mainly in about the last twenty years of the 20th century. If the work is to be distributed electronically, the final files are saved as formats appropriate to the target operating systems of the hardware used for reading. These may include PDF files.

Sales and marketing stage

The sales and marketing stage is closely intertwined with the editorial process. As front cover images are produced or chapters are edited, sales people may start talking about the book with their customers to build early interest. Publishing companies often produce advanced information sheets that may be sent to customers or overseas publishers to gauge possible sales. As early interest is measured, this information feeds back through the editorial process and may affect the formatting of the book and the strategy employed to sell it. For example, if interest from foreign publishers is high, co-publishing deals may be established whereby publishers share printing costs in producing large print runs thereby lowering the per-unit cost of the books. Conversely, if initial feedback is not strong, the print-run of the book may be reduced, the marketing budget cut or, in some cases, the book is dropped from publication altogether.

Printing

After the end of editing and design work the printing phase begins. The first step involves the production of a pre-press proof, which the printers send for final checking and sign-off by the publisher. This proof shows the book precisely as it will appear once printed and represents the final opportunity for the publisher to find and correct any errors. Some printing companies use electronic proofs rather than printed proofs. Once the publisher has approved the proofs, printing – the physical production of the printed work – begins. A new printing process has emerged as printing on demand. The book is written, edited, and designed as usual, but it is not printed until the publisher receives an order for the book from a customer. This procedure ensures low costs for storage, and reduces the likelihood of printing more books than will be sold.

Binding

In the case of books, binding follows upon the printing process. It involves folding the printed sheets, "securing them together, affixing boards or sides thereto, and covering the whole with leather or other materials"

Distribution

The final stage in publication involves making the product available to the public, usually by offering it for sale. In previous centuries, authors frequently also acted as their own editor, printer, and bookseller, but these functions have generally become separated. Once a book, newspaper, or other publication is printed, the publisher may use a variety of channels to distribute it. Books are most commonly sold through booksellers and through other retailers. Newspapers and magazines are typically sold in advance directly by the publisher to subscribers, and then distributed either through the postal system or by newspaper carriers. Periodicals are also frequently sold through newsagents and vending machines. Within the book industry, printers often fly some copies of the finished book to publishers as sample copies to aid sales or to be sent out for pre-release reviews. The remaining books often travel from the printing facility via sea freight. Accordingly, the delay between the approval of the pre-press proof and the arrival of books in a warehouse, much less in a retail store, can take some months. For books that tie into movie release-dates (particularly for children's films), publishers will arrange books to arrive in store up to two months prior to the movie release in order to build interest in the movie.

Publishing as a business

Derided in the 1911 Encyclopedia Britannica as "a purely commercial affair" that cared more about profits than about literary quality, publishing is fundamentally a business, with a need for the expenses of creating, producing, and distributing a book or other publication not to exceed the income derived from its sale. Publishing is now a major industry with the largest companies Reed Elsevier and Pearson PLC having global publishing operations. The publisher usually controls the advertising and other marketing tasks, but may subcontract various aspects of the process to specialist publisher marketing agencies. In many companies, editing, proofreading, layout, design and other aspects of the production process are done by freelancers. Dedicated in-house salespeople are sometimes replaced by companies who specialize in sales to bookshops, wholesalers and chain stores for a fee. This trend is accelerating as retail book chains and supermarkets have centralized their buying. If the entire process up to the stage of printing is handled by an outside company or individuals, and then sold to the publishing company, it is known as book packaging. This is a common strategy between smaller publishers in different territorial markets where the company that first buys the intellectual property rights then sells a package to other publishers and gains an immediate return on capital invested. Indeed, the first publisher will often print sufficient copies for all markets and thereby get the maximum quantity efficiency on the print run for all.

Some businesses maximize their profit margins through vertical integration; book publishing is not one of them. Although newspaper and magazine companies still often own printing presses and binderies, book publishers rarely do. Similarly, the trade usually sells the finished products through a distributor who stores and distributes the publisher's wares for a percentage fee or sells on a sale or return basis. The advent of the Internet has provided the electronic way of book distribution without the need of physical printing, physical delivery and storage of books. This therefore poses an interesting question that challenges publishers, distributors and retailers. The question pertains to the role and importance the publishing houses have in the overall publishing process. It is a common practice that the author, the original creator of the work, signs the contract awarding him or her only around

10% of the proceeds of the book. Such contract leaves 90% of the book proceeds to the publishing houses, distribution companies, marketers and retailers. One example (rearranged) of the distribution of proceeds from the sale of a book was given as follows:

- 45% to the retailer

- 10% to the wholesaler

- 10.125% to the publisher for printing (this is usually subcontracted out)

- 7.15% to the publisher for marketing

- 12.7% to the publisher for pre-production

- 15% to the author (royalties)

There is a common misconception that publishing houses make large profits, and that authors are the lowest paid in the publishing chain. However, most publishers make little profit from individual titles, with 75% of books not breaking even. Approximately 80% of the cost of a book is taken up by the expenses of preparing, distributing and printing (with printing being one of the lowest costs of all). On successful titles, publishing companies will usually make around 10% profit, with the author(s) receiving 8-15% of the retail price. However, given that authors are usually individuals, are often paid advances irrespective of whether the book turns a profit, and do not normally have to split profits with others, it makes them the highest paid individuals in the publishing process. Within the electronic book path, the publishing house's role remains almost identical. The process of preparing a book for e-book publication is exactly the same as print publication, with only minor variations in the process to account for the different mediums of publishing. While some costs, such as the discount given to retailers (normally around 45% are eliminated, additional costs connected to ebooks apply (especially in the conversion process), raising the production costs to a similar level.

Print on demand is rapidly becoming an established alternative to traditional publishing. In 2005, Amazon.com announced its purchase of Booksurge and selfsanepublishing, a major print on demand operation. This is probably intended as a preliminary move towards establishing an Amazon imprint. CreateSpace is the Amazon subsidiary that facilitates publishing by small presses and individual authors. Books published via create space are sold on Amazon and other outlets, with Amazon extracting a very high percentage of the sales proceeds for the services of publishing. printing and distributing. One of the largest bookseller chains, Barnes & Noble, already runs its own successful imprint with both new titles and classics — hardback editions of out-of-print former best sellers. Similarly, Ingram Industries, parent company of Ingram Book Group (a leading US book wholesaler), now includes its own print-on-demand division called Lightning Source. In 2013, Ingram launched a small press and self publishing arm called Ingram Spark. Payment terms are much closer to those of Amazon and less favorable than those they offer to more established publishers via Lightning Source. Among publishers, Simon & Schuster recently announced that it will start selling its backlist titles directly to consumers through its website. Book clubs are almost entirely direct-to-retail, and niche publishers pursue a mixed strategy to sell through all available outlets — their output is insignificant to the major booksellers, so lost revenue poses no threat to the traditional symbiotic relationships between the four activities of printing, publishing, distribution and retail.

INDUSTRY SUB-DIVISIONS

Newspaper publishing: Newspapers are regularly scheduled publications that present recent news, typically on a type of inexpensive paper called newsprint. Most newspapers are primarily sold to subscribers, through retail newsstands or are distributed as advertising-supported free newspapers. About one-third of publishers in the United States are newspaper publishers.

Periodical publishing: Nominally, periodical publishing involves publications that appear in a new edition on a regular schedule. Newspapers and magazines are both periodicals, but within the industry, the periodical publishing is frequently considered a separate branch that includes magazines and even academic journals, but not newspapers. About one-third of publishers in the United States publish periodicals (not including newspapers).

Book publishing: Book publishers represent less than a sixth of the publishers in the United States. Most books are published by a small number of very large book publishers, but thousands of smaller book publishers exist. Many small- and medium-sized book publishers specialize in a specific area. Additionally, thousands of authors have created their own publishing companies, and self-published their own works. Within the book publishing industry, the publisher of record for a book is the entity in whose name the book's ISBN is registered. The publisher of record may or may not be the actual publisher. Approximately 60% of English-language books are produced through the "Big Five" publishing houses: Penguin Random House, Hachette, HarperCollins, Simon & Schuster and Macmillan.

Directory publishing: Directory publishing is a specialized genre within the publishing industry. These publishers produce mailing lists, telephone books, and other types of directories.[9] With the advent of the Internet, many of these directories are now online.

Academic publishing: Academic publishers are typically either book or periodical publishers that have specialized in academic subjects. Some, like university presses, are owned by scholarly institutions. Others are commercial businesses that focus on academic subjects. The development of the printing press represented a revolution for communicating the latest hypotheses and research results to the academic community and supplemented what a scholar could do personally. But this improvement in the efficiency of communication created a challenge for libraries, which have had to accommodate the weight and volume of literature. One of the key functions that academic publishers provide is to manage the process of peer review. Their role is to facilitate the impartial assessment of research and this vital role is not one that has yet been usurped, even with the advent of social networking and online document sharing. Today, publishing academic journals and textbooks is a large part of an international industry. Critics claim that standardised accounting and profit-oriented policies have displaced the publishing ideal of providing access to all. In contrast to the commercial model, there is non-profit publishing, where the publishing organization is either organised specifically for the purpose of publishing, such as a university press, or is one of the functions of an organisation such as a medical charity, founded to achieve specific practical goals. An alternative approach to the corporate model is open access, the online distribution of individual articles and academic journals without charge to readers and libraries. The pioneers of Open Access journals are BioMed Central and the Public Library of Science (PLoS). Many commercial publishers are experimenting with hybrid models where older articles or government funded articles are made free, and newer articles are available as part of a subscription or individual article purchase.

Tie-in publishing

Technically, radio, television, cinemas, VCDs and DVDs, music systems, games, computer hardware and mobile telephony publish information to their audiences. Indeed, the marketing of a major film often includes a novelization, a graphic novel or comic version, the soundtrack album, a game, model, toys and endless promotional publications. Some of the major publishers have entire divisions devoted to a single franchise, e.g. Ballantine Del Rey Lucasbooks has the exclusive rights to Star Wars in the United States; Random House UK (Bertelsmann)/Century LucasBooks holds the same rights in the United Kingdom. The game industry self-publishes through BL Publishing/Black Library (Warhammer) and Wizards of the Coast (Dragonlance, Forgotten Realms, etc.). The BBC has its own publishing division that does very well with long-running series such as Doctor Who. These multimedia works are cross-marketed aggressively and sales frequently outperform the average stand-alone published work, making them a focus of corporate interest.

Independent publishing alternatives

Writers in a specialized field or with a narrower appeal have found smaller alternatives to the mass market in the form of small presses and self-publishing. More recently, these options include print on demand and eBook format. These publishing alternatives provide an avenue for authors who believe that mainstream publishing will not meet their needs or who are in a position to make more money from direct sales than they could from bookstore sales, such as popular speakers who sell books after speeches. Authors are more readily published by this means due to the much lower costs involved.

Recent developments

The 21st century has brought a number of new technological changes to the publishing industry. These changes include e-books, print on demand and accessible publishing. E-books have been quickly growing in availability in major publishing markets such as the USA and the UK since 2005. Google, Amazon.com and Sony have been leaders in working with publishers and libraries to digitize books. As of early 2011 Amazon's Kindle reading device is a significant force in the market, along with the Apple iPod and the Nook from Barnes & Noble.[citation needed] Along with the growing popularity of e-books, some companies like Oyster and Scribed have pursued the subscription model, providing members unlimited access to a content library on a variety of digital reading devices. The ability to quickly and cost-effectively print on Demand has meant that publishers no longer have to store books at warehouses, if the book is in low or unknown demand. This is a huge advantage to small publishers who can now operate without large overheads and large publishers who can now cost-effectively sell their backlisted items.

Accessible publishing uses the digitization of books to mark up books into XML and then produces multiple formats from this to sell to consumers, often targeting those with difficulty reading. Formats include a variety larger print sizes, specialized print formats for dyslexia, eye tracking problems and macular degeneration, as well as Braille, DAISY, audiobooks and e-books. Green publishing means adapting the publishing process to minimize environmental impact. One example of this is the concept of on-demand printing, using digital or print-on-demand technology. This cuts down the need to ship books since they are manufactured close to the customer on a just-in-time basis. A further development is the growth of on-line publishing where no physical books are produced. The eBook is created by the author and uploaded to a website from where it can be downloaded and read by anyone. An increasing number of small authors are using niche marketing online to sell more books by engaging with their readers online. These authors can use free services such as Smash words or Amazon's Creates pace to have their book available for worldwide sale. There is an obvious attraction for first time authors who have been repeatedly rejected by the existing agent/publisher model to explore this opportunity. However a consequence of this change in the mechanics of book distribution is that there is now no mandatory check on author skill or even their ability to spell, and any person with an internet connection can publish whatever they choose, regardless of the literary merit or even basic readability of their writing.

Standardization: Refer to the ISO divisions of ICS 01.140.40 and 35.240.30 for further information.

Legal issues: Publication is the distribution of copies or content to the public. The Berne Convention requires that this can only be done with the consent of the copyright holder, which is initially always the author. In the Universal Copyright Convention, "publication" is defined in article VI as "the reproduction in tangible form and the general distribution to the public of copies of a work from which it can be read or otherwise visually perceived. In providing a work to the general public, the publisher takes responsibility for the publication in a way that a mere printer or a shopkeeper does not. For example, publishers may face charges of defamation, if they produce and distribute libelous material to the public, even if the libel was written by another person.

Prevising: Prevising (private publishing) is a recently coined term for publishing a book in such a small amount, or with such lack of marketing, advertising or sales support from the publisher, that the book effectively does not reach the public. The book, while nominally published, is almost impossible to obtain through normal channels such as bookshops, often cannot be special-ordered and will have a notable lack of support from its publisher, including refusals to reprint the title. A book that is prevised may be referred to as "killed". Depending on the motivation, prevising may constitute breach of contract, censorship, or good business practice (e.g., not printing more books than the publisher believes will sell in a reasonable length of time).

CHAPTER 11:
CLOSING THE BOOK ON YOUR BOOK: A NEW BEGINNING

WRITING AND FINALIZING A BEST SELLER BOOK

Many a budding author dreams of writing the book, the one that turns into a bestseller, it's the book that gets you known and paid well. Not having written a bestseller yet doesn't necessarily show a lack of talent because there are tricks to making bestsellers, and it's not always stuff that sits well with the pure artist, like being trendy and being able to let go and let the editors have their own way with your writing. Provided you're made of stern enough stuff though, why not give the bestseller track a chance––you just never know.

Fiction or non-fiction

Decide which area of writing works best for you. If you're flexible, maybe try both. You never know which might work best. The next steps provide the things to consider in making your choice.

Choose fiction: Take a look at How to write a short story and its related for detailed assistance. Prepare the profile and the background of your characters in advance. The would-be bestseller must be easy to read and:

- Your readers must be able to sequence the events from earliest to latest; a reader will quickly give up if they are all mixed up and unclear.

- Your readers must be able to tell in what sequence the events in your book 'occurred'.

- In general, infinitely super-glue the attention of your readers through connecting traits in your characters, amazing plots and fascinating story-telling.

Choose non-fiction. Look for a relevant topic that a great many people are concerned about. You have two angles: find out whether anybody has yet written about it. No? Great, go for it. Yes? What unique angle can you provide that hasn't yet been covered?

- Refer to as many useful sources as possible on the topic.

Think mish mash: Who says this bestseller has to be a novel or a non-fiction style? It might be a blog, an autobiography, a travel-log, an esteemed reference text, a children's book, a school textbook (captive audience, bound to be a bestseller) or a book of fierce humor. It might be other [insert here]. Choose whatever style works for your quirks and abilities and run with it, right to the many publishing methods now available to you.

Select your topic: In general, selection of the topic will be helped by some or all of the following:

- You're passionate about the topic. You could write on it until the cows come home and then some.

- It's a really popular topic, either currently (get moving then) or perennially (always have a unique angle though).

If you're writing fiction, some additional helpers include:

- You already know your characters inside out and think you've met them personally. Writing about them will be a breeze.

- You have a plethora of current day fixations, addictions and fascinations in your notebook, waiting to fly off the page and accost your characters and mess up their lives. People love to be able to connect with the everyday stuff that rankles, perplexes and overwhelms.

If you're writing non-fiction, the following also tends to help:

- It's something you're an expert at/in. Or you are willing to research it to death. Nicer still if you have a certificate or degree or oodles of experience to back up this expertise and/or research. It helps people feel that you're reliable.

- You have the phone numbers of experts you can call on to ask questions about when you're stuck or feel like making it up.

- You like what you're writing about. If not, you're very good at standing in the shoes of different perspectives and you're able to remain objective. How long you can keep that up will determine how successful you'll be at getting the book completed.

WRITING THE BOOK

Take notes all the time. Carry a notebook with you wherever you go and capture the ideas that pop into your head at the time they appear. Find the time to write, few people can afford to be novelists-in-residence without some income source earned by fair means or foul. Unless you're Alain de Botton, who writes living off an inheritance (although now his writing makes the money too), you'd best make the time wherever it's free. Use your time on the bus to and from work, during lunch, after dinner, on the weekends, during vacation blocks. Asking for time off work to write a bestseller should be done with care, Judge the nature of your workplace first––the more conservative the establishment, the less likely this will be something considered worth their loss of your time. Be focused on the purpose of this book. Bestsellers do not need to be the best written, some may well be, but it can also take many years before the public catches up with such genius unless you also manage to win a literary prize. If you want to be great now, just start typing or writing, get it down and then fiddle with it later. Procrastination and perfection are the enemies of the bestseller.

Write a synopsis of your book: A plan, an outline, whatever you will. You can mind map it if you prefer. There are lots of rules for doing this. You can even read those too if you like. Or you can just get stuck into it and write, write, write. Not everyone does this the color-by-numbers way, so find your own path.

Fiction: Set out the characters, their traits and quirks, their motivations. This should be fun; fill them out as they grow in your mind. If they're based on your neighbor or ex-lover, make sure they're unrecognizable unless you enjoy being sued. And write out the situations you want to develop in your book, the plot so to speak, the series of events, be they fortunate or not so fortunate. And how will this all end? A cliffhanger, a surprise, a happy ending or a kaboom and everyone dies?

Non-fiction: Consider the need for sections, methods, parts––how will you break things down? Chapters can be nested inside sections, etc. Say you're writing about people's love of apple pies. Section one could cover what the apple pie is, with stories of people waxing nostalgic about apple pies from years gone by. Section two is where to source the best apples for pie making. Section three is a stack of apple pie recipes. Section four is troubleshooting failed apple pies. Section five is photos of your favorite apple pies off Instagram. And so forth... Some topics, like cats and beer, people will never get enough of and all you need to do is have a modern, current angle. Other things that are way too cliched, like celebrities and pop music, and you'll need funky new ways of bringing such over-written topics to people's attention that they don't already know.

Review progress frequently: Is the writing taking you where you want it to? Is it good, interesting, fathomable, fascinating, gripping, useful, entertaining, sparkling, witty, trendy, or whatever combination of such things you're trying to make it? Don't be afraid of splitting elements off for other projects. Sometimes you are mid-stream writing about one thing and another insists on birthing itself. Write it down, label it and put it aside for your next project. Avoid trying to add too much to the one piece you're writing now. After all, should you manage the bestseller, you'll need to produce more after and these side ideas are perfect germs of new bestsellers for later.

Set a deadline. Miss it various times. Set more deadlines. Miss those too. After all, life has a habit of getting in the way. Eventually, set the uncrossable deadline and mean it. This time, finish the book. Enough already! There is a point at which you must choose between being an author-in-waiting and a published-author-hoping-for-a-bestseller. Decide and get on with the writing to completion.

Be realistic. A book on the lost herd of rice carving gnus of outer Mongolia will likely take longer than a fiction piece about vampires destroying the local tea party. Especially if you need to budget the money and travel to outer Mongolia to verify the research. Deep research can take years; you can nudge your imagination quite a bit faster.

Holes can be filled in later. That is what friendly reviewers and your not-so-friendly editors are for, pre-publication. Listen to them; they can see the trees you keep missing for being deep in the proverbial

REVIEWING THE WRITING

Go over the work thoroughly. Read your own work after a break. Correct grammatical and spelling errors. Remove stuff that is fluff, bloat, nonsense or simply adds nothing special. Have the work reviewed by colleagues, coworkers, acquaintances. While you may be tempted to get friends and family to review it, do you really believe they'll be able to tell you honest irritation, dislike or criticism? Be fair on them and realistic and only ask people who are less inclined to flatter you or be subjective. For example, you may join a writer's club and meet a few critics who are able to give you suggestions on improvement.

Try to come up with a unique or catchy title for your book. As a case in point, if your book is about global warming, the title can be 'Coats are Useless': The uselessness of coats indicate the impossibility of winter since we wear coats in winter. However, avoid getting stuck on this aspect. Many an author wastes time trying to come up with the perfect title, only to have the publisher hate it and change it anyway. Put some effort into the title but not all your spare time.

Submit your book to a journalist who has a good reputation (who does not trample authors' work). Maybe this does not seem specific. You can have your book listed in a catalog or you can write to a newspaper/magazine to advertise your book. Better bring along positive comments from other reputable magazines and/or critics.

Be humble: Let your editors rip the work to pieces. Don't pontificate about how amazing your writing is. Editors are crafts persons just like writers and they are there to help not hinder you. They are there to polish the gems and bring them to their shiny potential, hopefully bestselling potential. Embrace this help for all it is worth and let them make their suggestions. Entertain their suggestions seriously. Friendly editors are useful for easing you into the editing experience. Nasty ones are just nasty and are good for sharpening your wits against and allowing you some self pity. At the end of the day though, look for the ones in between--nice to invite to a dinner party but very fierce about their craft and the ability to make your craft look better. Submit the book to a publisher only if you do not mind having the book edited impersonally. This can be a good or a bad thing, depending on how you choose to view it. On the whole, the experience of that editor and the backing of a publishing house and its already established reputation can only be good for you. There are people who purchase based on who published the book, not just who wrote it.

Make essential changes. Ultimately, you need to make good judgment calls about what to leave in, what to rewrite and what to pull out, based on your editor's and reviewer's comments. Trust both your own instincts and what they have said, but be careful about both. Your own instinct can sometimes just be stubbornness parading as "truth", while not every reviewer or editor will get the totality of your writing. Try to get some distance from the writing, give yourself time to consider the comments made about it, then come back to it and assemble it for its last phase, the publication.

PUBLISHING AND WAITING...

Decide how the book will be published. There are different possibilities, such as using a renowned publisher, vanity publishing or publishing eBooks or blogs online. Choose a well known publisher and half the battle can be won for bestseller status. Suggested examples are Oxford University Press and Penguin Books, which publish many bestsellers. However, publishers reject a lot of attempts at book deals, so have a huge list to work through and don't give up. Keep sending that manuscript out, again and again until it gets accepted. If not, vanity publishing is more accessible than ever. Let the publisher do the marketing needed. If you've chosen to use an established publisher and they've accepted your work, expect them to market the daylights out of the book. If they don't, ask why not. If you don't like the answer, you might need to return to the drawing board but it is worth pushing them before giving up.

Wait:

Some bestsellers are sleepers. Some might need nudges from you. Share the link to where it can be bought from on Twitter, Facebook, Google+, etc. Give some away in blog or Facebook competitions. Tell friends and family it has been published (the one time you can guilt them into helping through this whole process). Give some away as Christmas gifts. Send copies to a favorite celebrity. Market yourself. Understand that there is no guarantee that the bestseller magic will happen. It completely depends on the situation, the whim of the buyers, the tone of the season, the calibration of the planet... Really, there are lots of things that go into making written work turn bestseller or viral. You can do your best to achieve this but apart from the well known (and very bankable) churner authors in such areas as crime, law and romance, most authors live with hope. Your publisher can do some things but even they can't perform miracles, so be patient. If, after a year or two, the book seems to be doing the ordinary thing, like being bought occasionally, go back and write again. It just means you've still got a bestseller waiting to emerge, so don't give up. Consider sending your book to literary award groups or organizations. In some cases, the publisher may need to do this on your behalf. Getting an award can be helpful though, both for recognition and a little bit of handy cash. Start writing the sequel, get onto this really quickly if your work is a bestseller; your readers are already hanging out for more. Ditto if it isn't a bestseller––the sooner you get back to believing in your writing, the better.

PROMOTING YOUR BOOK

So you have written a book and had it published. Congratulations. Now you face the challenge of what to do next. Many authors think that marketing is a job for the publisher so they sit back and wait for the royalties to roll in. You might have a very long wait. The market for books is extremely crowded and most books do not sell well. However, there are a number of things that the author can do that will really help so make the move from writing to marketing and take these actions:

1. Send review copies to all the journals and magazines that review books in your genre. This is something that most publishers do for you but there is no harm in sharing lists and helping out. If you have self-published you will certainly have to focus on this. Don't forget the many online sites that review books.

2. Get friends, colleagues, clients or anyone who likes your book to place reviews on Amazon and other online book stores. Amazon is highly influential and the reviews matter so encourage anyone who says they enjoyed your book to place a review.

3. Offer yourself for interview on radio stations. Most radio stations are looking for interesting interviews and the author of a newly published book has a good chance of getting on air. You need a publicity letter which says something interesting or controversial about the book and off you go. If you have the budget you can use a professional PR company to target radio and TV programs.

4. Create a web page for the book. Ideally you should have a separate website with an address that features the book title. Now you can exchange links and drive traffic to the site with comments, blogs, quotes and extracts. Be sure to show people how they can buy the book. Encourage user feedback, comments and reviews.

5. Offer sample chapters as free downloads. Take a couple of your best chapters and turn them into pdf files. Let people download them for free. Think of this as the equivalent of letting people browse through your book at a bookstore.

6. Use material from the book in your blog. Start a blog and quote from the book. Lift sections and acknowledge the book as the source. Build a community of interest around the topics in the book.

7. Review other books in this field. Become a reviewer on Amazon. Use your own name accompanied by 'author of the book. Review other books and when people read your reviews some will click through to your book.

8. Start an email newsletter. Encourage people to subscribe on the website and then send out an occasional newsletter with interesting new material in this book's field. But you cannot just plug your book – you have to add value with new information and comment.

9. Give away copies to the right people. Use the book as your calling card. Give copies

to potential and existing clients. Encourage them to read it and pass it on.

10. Offer books as prizes. Local radio shows, magazines or societies will often be interested in running competitions and will give you valuable publicity if you give them a few books to give away as prizes.

Some authors do book signings in local bookstores but, unless you are very well-known, this activity is unlikely to produce worthwhile results. Finally, you could consider using the book as a platform for launching your speaking career. You will need a different set of skills to succeed here but the book can make an excellent starting point and every talk will help sell more books.